Sandra Wilde

Funner Grammar

GRADES 3–8

FRESH WAYS to Teach Usage, Language, and Writing Conventions

HEINEMANN
Portsmouth, NH

Heinemann
361 Hanover Street
Portsmouth, NH 03801–3912
www.heinemann.com
Offices and agents throughout the world

Library of Congress Cataloging-in-Publication Data

Wilde, Sandra.
   Funner grammar : fresh ways to teach usage, language, and writing conventions, grades 3–8 / Sandra Wilde.
        pages   cm
   Includes bibliographical references.
   ISBN 978-0-325-01392-3
   ISBN 0-325-01392-6
  1. Language arts (Elementary).   2. English language—Grammar—Study and teaching (Elementary).   I. Title.
   LB1576.W487657 2012
   372.6—dc23   2012003393

Editor: Tina Miller
Production: Patricia Adams
Cover and Interior Designs: Lisa Fowler
Typesetter: Eric Rosenbloom, Kirby Mountain Composition
Manufacturing: Steve Bernier

Printed in the United States of America on acid-free paper

16 15 14 13 12 ML 1 2 3 4 5

To the students—past, present, and future—
of Anicinabe Community School, on the north shore of
Sagkeeng First Nation in Manitoba, Canada,
where I began my teaching career.

And to Noam Chomsky,
for the insights and inspiration he's provided
for all of my work in language.

At Heinemann: First and foremost, editor Tina Miller, who asked if she could work with me on this project and has been smart and delightful and patient. Production coordinator Patty Adams, who's efficient and engaged and totally got what I was trying to do. Lisa Fowler, designer of both the text and cover, who has a playful mind and figured out exactly what colors would work. Elizabeth Valway, who wrote the early promotion copy, and Eric Chalek, who did the later marketing. Freelance copyeditor David Cottingham, who combined a light hand and lapidary precision. Kate Montgomery, who kickstarted getting this book going again and thought the title was the bestest.

At Hunter College (City University of New York): all of my excellent colleagues within and beyond the Department of Curriculum and Teaching, particularly Dean David Steiner. My students, who continue to push my thinking, with a special shout-out to the students in Developmental Reading in the fall of 2011 who were the first ones to say that *Funner Grammar* rocked as a title. A number of classroom teachers contributed ideas and stories; they are mentioned throughout the book.

The students at PS 180 (Hugo Newman Preparatory School) in Harlem, who amaze me with their intellectual curiosity and give me new ideas every time I see them. Also the teachers I've worked with there, especially Carolyn Montalto and Stephanie Bailyn, and principal Peter (Dr. Mac) MacFarlane. I began work with PS 180 in 2004 on a sabbatical from Portland State University in Oregon, and now live less than a mile from it. Life is magical.

John McWhorter, who kindly replied to an out-of-the-blue email from a stranger and fan and made thoughtful comments on the manuscript.

Fellow grammar gal Jane Bean-Folkes; we help each other explore and challenge conventional wisdom. Donna Schrier, who is a continual fountain of wisdom about teaching.

Marcin Korzep and Chris Sosa, for helping to make my daily life easier. My doctors Adam Karp, MD, and Robert Lind, MD, for helping me stay healthy as I get older. Lauren Waine, for lots of help and support.

Finally, the eight million people of New York City, who make my life a daily delight and expose me to language variety beyond imagining. I talk to strangers and hear them talking on the subway and on the street. How lucky I am to live in this city.

Introduction

Did you know that there are about six thousand languages in the world? And that speakers of some 322 of them live in the United States? (www.usefoundation.org/userdata/file/Research/findings.pdf) Did you know that children in Los Angeles schools have been identified as speaking 92 languages? Did you know that there are 180 Native American languages still spoken in this country (http://spinner.cofc.edu/linguist/archives/2005/06/how_many_native.html), but that many of them are facing extinction? Did you know that about 28 million residents of the United States speak Spanish? Did you know how rapidly English is spreading throughout the world, to the point that there's a book about it called *Globish* (McCrum, 2010)?

And did you know that, like every language, English is changing all the time? Chaucer's English is almost impossible for us to read today, Shakespeare's is challenging,[1] and *Peter Pan* is difficult, but today's prize-winning fiction is pulling language from today's America and projecting it into the future. Here's a sentence from page 3 of Junot Diaz's 2008 Pulitzer Prize winner for fiction, *The Brief Wondrous Life of Oscar Wao*, set among Dominican-

---

[1] Linguist John McWhorter (1998), for instance, thinks that Shakespeare should be translated, preferably by poets, into contemporary language when his plays are performed; they're just too hard to follow.

Americans: "For what Kennedy's intelligence experts failed to tell him was what every single Dominican, from the richest jabao in Mao to the poorest güey in El Buey, from the oldest anciano sanmacorisano to the littlest cajaristo in San Francisco, knew: that whoever killed Trujillo, their family would suffer a fukú so dreadful it would make the one that attached itself to the Admiral jojote in comparison." Not your grandfather's Pulitzer Prize winner, is it?[2] Jennifer Egan's 2010 Pulitzer Prize winner, *A Visit from the Goon Squad*, ends with a chapter set in the 2020s, where she imagines what texting (or, as the characters refer to it, T) will look like in the future: "u herd th nUs?/Nu job .in the wrks - big $ pos. pls kEp opn mind."

So what does this have to do with teaching grammar? Everything. The teaching of grammar has traditionally been about teaching kids to speak and write "correctly"; it has largely fallen out of favor, but teachers often feel they should be doing something with grammar, and will soon feel pressured to do so as the new Common Core State Standards (CCSS) for grades K–12 (2010), including language standards, are adopted by more and more states. It won't surprise me if your reaction is "Ew, grammar." Many of us have our bad grammar stories, don't we? Unless you're too young to have experienced grammar curriculum in school, you may have memories like mine, in which I'm sitting in Mr. Strub's classroom in Plainfield High School as we drone our way through interminable exercises from Warriner's *English Grammar and Composition*. Compound and complex sentences, subjects and predicates, *lie* and *lay*.

> It won't surprise me if your reaction is "Ew, grammar."

But hooray, grammar, too. My good grammar stories are about learning how language really works, how verb tenses in English are a lot more elegant

---

2 ⊢ Here, by contrast, is a passage that's from your great-grandfather's (i.e., 1918) Pulitzer winner, from the first page of *His Family*, by Ernest Poole: "A place of turbulent thoroughfares, of shouting drivers, hurrying crowds, the crack of whips and the clatter of wheels; an uproarious thrilling town of enterprise, adventure, youth; a city of pulsing energies, the center of a boundless land; a port of commerce with all the world; of stately ships with snowy sails; a fascinating pleasure town, with throngs of eager travellers hurrying from the ferry boats and rolling off in hansom cabs to the huge hotels on Madison Square." (Note that this sentence from the first page of the first novel to win the Pulitzer is technically a fragment.) The Diaz sentence has 66 words and the Poole one 79; both are complex, excellent sentences, and each reflects its era.

than the names we learned for them; how sign language is a real language, not just a series of gestures; how scientists tried to teach language to chimps and gorillas but failed. I hope this book will inspire you to realize that what we should be helping kids to learn about isn't traditional grammar, but fresh, new grammar, all the strange and wonderful knowledge and information about language that makes it as fun as any other human topic to learn about. In doing so, I hope to frame a discussion about looking at language as a human social phenomenon, one that's closely tied to history and culture, and that's also a tool for connecting with people in speech and writing. Language is a birthright of every human being, in the sense that everyone (barring some disabilities) acquires language (spoken or signed), and that no culture does it wrong, no languages or dialects are superior to others, and we all own language and have the opportunity to make of it what we wish and get better at expressing ourselves and our ideas with it. I also want to show you how to help kids pass grammar tests and learn to use the language of power (especially because some will have a head start over others because of accidents of birth).

On the practical side, I'll be suggesting, and laying out explicitly, what grammar you should teach given the huge number of topics that you *could* teach: yes, kids should learn the names of the parts of speech, and as painlessly as possible; no, they don't need to be able to distinguish a past participle from a future progressive, just use them, which they already do.

I'm starting from a premise that it's all good, that American kids who are native speakers of English all speak equally well, and that English language learners aren't doing so badly either. This point may be a hard sell, so I'll explain what I mean by it and make my case, a case that's crucial to the rethinking of grammar teaching that I think educators need to do. First of all, this isn't just my own opinion, it's the standard view of linguists—scientists who study language for a living—and who believe it's inarguable and obvious that everyone's language is equally good. This doesn't mean that speech errors don't exist, merely that the speech patterns of any human community are equally good, correct, valid, and legitimate. In the words of Steven Pinker, you'd never hear the narrator of a nature documentary say that "the song of the humpback whale contains several well-known errors, and monkeys' cries have been in a state of chaos and degeneration for hundreds of years" (1995, p. 382). This doesn't mean that people don't *think* that other people don't talk right; but that's another issue, which we'll discuss in detail later. But for now I'd like to try to convince you that there's nothing inherently wrong with *ain't*, *talkin'*, *me and Bobby went out*, or other so-called grammatical errors. This is a necessary context for the rest of this book.

Let's look far back and deep, to how, where, and when language started. We know a lot about the history of written language, since much of it is preserved, but not so much about spoken language. There are a lot of different theories, so I'm going to focus on what we know with as much certitude as possible. The chances are good that the genetic capacity for language evolved only once, in Africa, around 50,000 years ago,[3] and then migrated in the group that then populated the rest of the world. The original human population at that time was as small as 2,000 to 5,000 people (http://en.wikipedia.org/wiki/Recent_African_origin_of_modern_humans). Is there an oldest language? Well, no, no more than there's an oldest human group. All of us, and all of our languages,[4] are descended from that first group in Africa.

Over time and space, language changed and its speakers migrated. Latin came along; the Latin spoken in Italy changed into Italian, while the Latin spoken elsewhere became French, Spanish, Portuguese, and Romanian. The French spoken by emigrants who moved to North America and the Caribbean became Canadian French and French-based creoles, all of them equally valid. France-based French isn't "better" than Canadian French any more than Italian is a better language than French because its precursor started in Italy. The people who stayed home don't speak the language better than those who moved away; language changes regardless of where its speakers live, and language diverges when its speakers no longer live close to each other. (If the version of a language in the place where it originated were

---

[3] ⊢ Different sources mention slightly different date ranges, usually in the vicinity of 50–70,000 years, because we don't know for sure. I'm going to use 50,000 throughout for simplicity.

[4] ⊢ This technically isn't 100 percent true; we *can* talk about newest languages. Nicaraguan sign developed spontaneously in an orphanage in the 1970s and is unrelated to other languages. More on this later.

the best version, African languages would trump all the other languages in the world.)

Let's think about language in the early days of America. The myth is that the founders of America were English speakers from Great Britain, but that's true only if we look at the history of the United States as a political entity. If we look back at the population three centuries ago, of all the territory that later became the United States, there were speakers of indigenous languages (including Polynesians in Hawaii), Spanish speakers (who were descendants of both Spaniards and indigenous people from what is now Mexico), and slaves who spoke many African languages, as well as people of varied social classes from the British isles and France. English of course became the dominant language over time, but the other languages persisted to different extents and influenced American English as it evolved.

Fast-forward to today. America is populated by people and descendants of people from all over the world. Of today's three-year-olds living in America in 2009, only 49.9 percent are white (extrapolated from Census Bureau Data by the Brookings Institution: www.brookings.edu/opinions/2011/0207_population_frey.aspx), and of those, of course, only some smaller percentage are descendants of people from England. So whose English do we speak? Well, everybody's, not just those of the earliest settlers from England. There *is* evidence that there's some type of Standard American English out there (although it's different for speech and for writing), but it's not as clear-cut and simple as it may seem. Let's look at three recent American presidents, all of them natural-born citizens whose language hasn't been a barrier to achievement at the highest levels.

Bill Clinton is from Arkansas, and you can still hear it in his speech. George W. Bush grew up in Texas and, despite his family's WASP Northeastern origins and his own prep school and Yale education, still sounds somewhat Texan. Barack Obama identifies and is seen as African American, but was raised in Hawaii and overseas largely by his white mother and grandparents. His public speech sounds generically American to most of us, although almost certainly he speaks African American English, which he was likely to have used in his work as a community organizer on the South Side of

Chicago.[5] These highly educated, high-achieving Americans have risen to positions of great power, and we tolerate slight lapses from Standard English in their speech. (I've heard all three of the men dropping *g*'s in their speech, although not Hillary Clinton.) They presumably speak differently in their private lives than in their public appearances; all three, for instance, have been known to use four-letter words.

Times have changed. I remember news media's discussion of whether Jimmy Carter's Southern accent would prejudice voters against him; Lyndon Johnson presumably only got a pass on his Texas accent because he'd been thrust into the presidency, but it was still seen in many quarters as a mark of ignorance. Today, Princeton Professor Cornel West intentionally speaks in the cadences of Black English in his scholarly presentations. One of the plays nominated for Broadway's 2011 Tony Awards is *The _____ With the Hat* (as the *New York Times* refers to it), written in rich, contemporary New York urban language, full of slang and cursing, much of it with a Puerto Rican influence. Sarah Palin's folksy language is seen by many voters as evidence of her connection with everyday Americans. *West Side Story*'s latest Broadway incarnation had dialogue and songs in both English and Spanish. Watch an American comedy from the 1930s and listen to how almost British the characters sound. Then watch a contemporary comedy and hear the slang and language play. (*Clueless*, 1995, is a classic example of a movie that not only used a lot of slang but perhaps invented some. The movie was based on the Jane Austen novel *Emma*; I found this guide to the slang of the movie created by the Jane Austen Society of Australia: www.jasa.net.au/study/cslang.htm.) One hears people using all kinds of language on the job; my recent mortgage loan officer says *aks*; the flight attendant on my plane recently referred to the passengers as "you guys," and the chief of hospital medicine at Montefiore Hospital was quoted in the *New York Times* as saying, "Me and my entire staff think it's important to answer [patient call buttons]" (May 30, 2011).

My larger point here? That American English is an amalgam of language throughout American history, linked to the British English (of a variety of so-

---

[5] I wrote to the White House to ask if he spoke it, but unsurprisingly didn't get a reply.

cial classes and regions) of the 17th and 18th centuries, but having grown and developed over some five centuries of use by Americans of diverse backgrounds. We could let kids know that people may look down on them if they say *ain't*, but how can we possibly claim that there's anything actually wrong with *ain't*, or with "can I?" rather than "may I?," or "The kids was playin'"? They're also not less logical than other forms, as we'll see later (including *ain't*). There are no grounds for criticizing these usages on their merits, since they're part of the everyday language of American speech communities, just like "She went to hospital when she got sick" (rather than *the* hospital) is everyday usage in Britain. To say otherwise is actually just snobbery, and it's also just not right that kids who speak this way should have diminished life chances, although it will serve them well to add features of standard American English for use in some situations.

So what next, as we think about grammar and language study for 21st-century America? We're working with kids who are all kinds of Americans. Some are native-born and some are immigrants. Those who are native-born are mostly descendants of immigrants from all over (only 7.7 percent of Americans claim ancestry from England, the ancestral home of our language, probably a lower percentage for children: http://en.wikipedia.org/wiki/Maps_of_American_ancestries), often from more than one country. Many of those immigrants came voluntarily, others involuntarily as slaves, still others escaping persecution in their original countries. Some of their roots are indigenous, from before the *Mayflower*, north or south of the Rio Grande. Students come from the whole range of social classes, which may or may not be the same as those of their grandparents (or their teachers). Many of them speak English as their first and probably their only language, some as their second or third or fourth, and some partially or not at all. And they're younger than us, which means their language is already different from ours. Each child who walks through a schoolhouse door is heading for a world where he'll be using language, spoken and written, to get through life and do well in ways that matter to him.

> So what next, as we think about grammar and language study for 21st-century America?

So what do these kids need from us? What do they need to know about language and be able to do with it linguistically, and what do you need to know to make that happen? I'm proposing that teachers approach the topic of language in the classroom by focusing on five areas: the linguistic conventions of written language (mechanics); how to talk about how language is put together (which I'm calling nitty-gritty grammar to distinguish it from the wider meaning of the term); what's considered right and wrong (usage); language prejudices (language and social justice); and learning interesting stuff about language (linguistics for kids). Each of these is the topic of one chapter of this book. Pretty much all of the old standbys of the grammar curriculum for these grade levels will turn up, but often seen from a new angle. For instance, curricula have often focused on formal teaching of topics like types of sentences, assuming that they have to be explicitly taught and learned; however, what if we wondered instead how kids *acquire* knowledge of compound and complex sentences, as seen in their writing?[6] This might well lead to a very different conception of the teacher's role.

I'm going to start in Chapter 2 with mechanics, used here to mean technical aspects of the writing process, because it's pretty straightforward. Often when I ask teachers what bothers them most about kids' grammar, they'll say that students don't know how to punctuate sentences, or they write in fragments, or write like they talk. In this chapter I'll sort out aspects of written language that contribute to making writing seem "correct," recognizing that the nature of good written language is to have well-formed sentences, punctuated appropriately, whose verb tenses hang together and parts fit together well. In some ways, learning this is a life's work, but we can identify parts of it that are age-appropriate and teachable for grades 3–8, also keeping in mind how to connect this work to the Common Core State Standards and to make it work for English language learners. Traditional grammar teaching was assumed to help students learn to write better, but research has proven this to

---

[6] This distinction between acquisition and learning of language was developed by Krashen (1981). *Acquiring* is picking up knowledge without consciously trying to, as when children begin talking; for instance, Hauser, Chomsky, and Fitch (2002) point out that the average high school graduate has acquired about 60,000 words with little effort. *Learning*, in the sense used here, involves an explicit intention, as in memorizing the multiplication tables.

be untrue; (Elley et al., 1975) however, there *is* a strong role for other kinds of teaching to deal with these more technical aspects of writing. I'll also mention relevant reference books for students and teachers.

Next, in Chapter 3, we'll look at the topics of traditional grammar instruction. A lot of it comes down to terminology and giving students a vocabulary to talk about language: what students should learn (if anything) about parts of speech, types of sentences, phrases and clauses, verb tenses, and so on. The CCSS are relevant here, and I'll also talk about what *not* to do. Many teachers who think they should be teaching grammar go to the Internet or to published materials to find lessons and exercises, but most of these resources are not only boring but useless. I expect more and more of these materials to be produced in the next few years because of the Common Core, and teachers need to be able to critique them and resist attempts to make them mandatory. You can help students pass any grammar tests that come along without recourse to using poor teaching materials. In this chapter I will, however, be spending some time on verb tenses, which are much more interesting than most people realize.

Then we'll move on, in Chapter 4, to the more complex topic of usage, which is what people are usually referring to when they talk about "bad grammar." We need to look at usage in all its social context; that is, why communities use somewhat different language to express the same ideas, specifically small differences in vocabulary and grammatical features like tense and suffixes. In doing so, I'll also talk about aspects of the CCSS that involve usage: what they mean, some ideas about why they might have been included in the standards, and how to think about them in work with students. Since the standards take a very traditional approach to usage, I'll be distinguishing between good teaching for learning about language, and also teaching to help kids do well on tests that reflect standards. For English language learners, traditional usage is all the more complicated, since it's already a lot of work just to learn English, let alone learn niceties that may not be part of the English they hear in the world around them.

Chapter 5 is about language and social justice. This grows out of the topic of usage, but also considers issues of helping children learn, and learn about, the language of power in American society. Because the language of some speakers is stigmatized, we have to think about why this is and what to do about it, including acknowledging and celebrating everybody's contributions to today's American English.

Finally, Chapter 6 is on linguistics as an object of study for children, with ideas about how to explore language in interesting ways. I've read a lot of books about language, and will include a Top Ten list for teachers who'd like to learn more. (For instance, what was the *real* story about Nim Chimpsky, the chimp who lived in an apartment in New York City where his trainers tried to teach him language?) But I'll also have teaching ideas. We can use digital resources here to help kids learn about the languages of the world, how English is used all over the world, and so on. Did you know, for example, that there's a blog of "unnecessary quotation marks"?

Lastly, some appendices: one with suggested units of study for different grade-level ranges, one summarizing how to work with the Common Core State Standards at each grade level, a style guide for students, some selections of suggested reading for teachers and kids, and thoughts on authentic representation of varieties of English. By the time you finish reading this book, you'll have a solid plan for spending an appropriate amount of time on language topics in ways that will move kids forward in their spoken and written expression, their ability to talk about language in technical ways using appropriate terminology, and their understanding of language in its social, cultural, and historical contexts.

CHAPTER 2

Mechanics

Conventions Found Only in Written Language

Spoken language is basic; writing involves extra knowledge. When we talk, words don't have spaces between them, sentences aren't always well formed, and our voices rise and fall without any punctuation marks. When we talk about grammar as part of the writing process—above and beyond what we notice in speech—we're often referring to mechanical issues, particularly punctuation but sometimes spelling, as when the writer means one word but writes another. Students need to be able to use conventions at the level of the word, clause, sentence, and larger discourse units, as well as special cases like writing dates and quotations.

Many of these conventions, such as the placement of apostrophes, follow rules, rules that are a mixture of logic and arbitrariness. Some of them can be written down very precisely (whether or not to capitalize *Earth*), others not so much (when is a sentence fragment acceptable?). Some vary depending on whose style manual you're using, such as APA and Chicago formats for bibliographic entries. They may vary depending on what you're writing: a text message, an email (and who's the recipient?[1]), a letter to the

---

[1] I can't help commenting on an edit I made here, since it's an example of how to use conventions intelligently rather than slavishly. I first wrote "who are you sending it to?," rejected a change of "to whom are you sending it?," then realized that rewording would be less stuffy but still not offend purists.

editor, a formal paper. We can also include issues of style and register, such as whether to be formal and use *whom*. Some mechanics questions have a clear right answer, and some don't. These conventions also change over time.

We also need to think about what level of proficiency we expect from students in grades 3–8. I've been dipping into Bryan Garner's splendid, thousand-page *Garner's Modern American Usage* (2009), and it makes distinctions that are valuable to me as someone who writes for publication,[2] but are way beyond what a 13-year-old should be expected to know. I visited a seventh-grade classroom whose teacher wanted me to explore quotation marks with the students. I soon discovered that they knew the basics. When we started getting into questions about where the punctuation marks go when you have a quotation inside a quotation and other special cases, I realized that they were at the level of knowing as much as anyone other than a copy editor needs to know. I think it makes sense to know the major rules, and then have style manuals and usage guides available to check if you aren't sure.

There are a lot of resources for teaching writing mechanics. What I propose to do in this chapter is provide a framework for exploring some key topics in grade-appropriate ways, by choosing facets of these conventions that are useful and amenable to teaching, starting at the word level and working up. I've done this in the form of ten lesson frameworks that I believe cover the basics of writing mechanics for grades 3–8, ending with a section on what not to teach and why. Four lessons are at the word level, two each at sentence and discourse level, and two are odds and ends. These topics are enough for a solid treatment of writing mechanics. I've also included appendices of resource books at the end of this book.

Is It the Right Word?

When we're talking, it doesn't always matter if we use exactly the right word. The verbs *affect* and *effect* sound the same, and we only feel insecure if we

---

2 For instance, when does *none* take a singular verb and when a plural one?

have to write them down. I hear teachers talk about (what sounds like) *pneu-monic devices* for remembering spelling, but no one else notices that they're saying a word meaning lung-related (as in *pneumonic* plague) rather than *mnemonic* (memory-related). In writing it would matter. The problem is in recognizing when you're using an "easily confused" word, precisely because they *are* easily confused. These two examples are spelling differences; others are more word choice, such as *disinterested* and *uninterested*. There are also "writing like you talk" cases, as when you write *gonna* or *alot*.

Three ideas for dealing with often-interchanged words. First, choose your battles. There are distinctions that aren't really maintained anymore; as a careful grammarian, you may be picky about the difference between *if* and *whether*, but most people don't have it on their radar. A copy editor would, and would catch it in proofreading a manuscript, but do 12-year-olds need to? It's easy to feel you're maintaining standards when really you're just trying to preserve usage distinctions that are fading from the language or possibly just your own pet peeves. Second, notice word-choice issues in your own stu-dents' writing and use them for brief lessons. (See Wilde, 2008, for instance, for a lesson on how to deal with homophone confusion.) There may be fewer than you think. And third, get a book on the topic to keep in your classroom. *100 Words Almost Everyone Confuses and Misuses* (American Heritage, 2004) has all the classic ones like *lie/lay, infer/imply, between/among.* Many of them are more precise than you'll need, but you and your students might enjoy browsing through it, and it would be a useful resource for lesson develop-ment. (See also Grammar Girl's similar book, Fogarty, 2011.)

Capital Letters

Sentences start with a capital letter. Well, duh. That's not the hard part; know-ing where the sentences break is the hard part. But let's think about capital letters in other cases. Merriam-Webster's *Pocket Guide to Punctuation* (2001) has 74 capitalization rules for proper nouns and adjectives. Teach one a day and you'll be done by winter break. No, just kidding! But did you know that *court* is sometimes capitalized in legal documents, particularly when written by the judge? (It is the opinion of this Court that . . . .) Here's a teaching idea, primarily for around third grade, that won't take much time. Keep a running list of categories of words that should be capitalized. (This actually works better than trying to define what a proper noun is; saying it's a specific person, place, or organization could lead kids to capitalize "my Teacher" but not "my dog rover.") You can start your list with names of people, pets, cities, states, and countries and add to it as the year goes on.

Capitalization might tie in to other areas of your curriculum as well. For instance, when you study astronomy: Should the names of the sun, earth, and moon be capitalized like the other major bodies in the solar system? Why or why not? (I'll let you research the answer yourself, but realize that style manuals may differ slightly from each other.) You could also ask students to keep an eye out for capitalized (or surprisingly uncapitalized) words when they read and ask you to explain or do a lesson on them. (Why do we capitalize *Dalmatian* but not *collie*?) The key is to help kids develop a theory of capitalization, thinking about which words are capitalized, and then to help them use reference books to find out in specific cases.

Apostrophes

Oh, apostrophes! Annoying little buggers, aren't they? You can't hear them, they're really confusing, and even adults have trouble with them. I see misused apostrophes out in the world all the time, most recently on a sign in front of TGIFriday's: "Margarita's/Cosmopolitan's/Long Island iced tea." Decades ago, I saw a large poster for a Canadian TV special, including, in large letters, the CBC network's slogan, "Television at it's [sic] best." Ouch. Proofreading at its worst.[3]

There are only six rules for apostrophe use (according to Merriam-Webster, 2001), so I'm going to tell you what they are: possessives; a few plurals (8's, *p*'s and *q*'s); contractions; representations of informal speech (*goin'*);

---

[3] Which reminds me of another (non-apostrophe) advertising blooper. I saw—one time only, before it was pulled—a full-page in-house ad in a newspaper: "The *Charlotte Observer*. It rubs off on you." They of course meant to refer to the power of its writing, not the quality of its ink.

omitted digits (spirit of '76); and forms of verbs based on letters (OK'd the deal). Why all the problems? Two reasons: confusing apostrophes and plurals, and confusing the contraction *it's* with the un-apostrophized possessive *its*.[4] These differences are easy to understand but also easy to confuse and are best dealt with through a simple lesson, ending with a clear statement, preferably in the students' own words, about when to use the apostrophe. This can then be posted as a proofreading guide. It may help to show a list of the possessive pronouns *his, hers, its, yours,* and *theirs.* They all end in *s,* but possessive pronouns never have apostrophes; the contraction of *it is* always has an apostrophe. Keep an eye out for these when you're proofreading; you'll always know how to fix them because the rule is straightforward.

Abbreviations, Acronyms, and Initialisms

This lesson is more for fun. We have a lot of short ways of writing and saying things. Abbreviations are usually written with a period and pronounced as a full word, like *Mr.* and *Oct.* Acronyms are words created from the initial letters of other words, and are often created intentionally as names of organizations, such as NOW, the National Organization for Women. There are also lowercase words that we don't even realize started out as acronyms, such as *laser,* "light amplification by the stimulated emission of radiation." (There are also unfortunate acronyms; you can enjoy examples at the blog Acronyms Sometimes Suck, although many of them can't be shared with children.) Initialisms are created from the initial letters of other words but are pronounced by saying the names of the letters, such as DVR (digital video recorder) and NBC (National

> There are also lowercase words that we don't even realize started out as acronyms, such as *laser,* "light amplification by the stimulated emission of radiation." (There are also unfortunate acronyms; you can enjoy examples at the blog Acronyms Sometimes Suck, although many of them can't be shared with children.)

---

[4] There are fine details about whether to add an *s* after the apostrophe for a possessive whose base word ends in *s* or *z,* but you can look them up if needed or not worry about them. There's also some variation; one usually writes Socrates' or Zeus's but always Jesus'. (The rule for why the period went outside the apostrophe at the end of the last sentence is also more than one needs to know for everyday writing.)

Broadcasting Company). Initialisms are of course rampant in text messaging and other new media, particularly when using a tiny keyboard or touch screen (lol, btw).

Merriam-Webster's punctuation guide (2001) has 21 pages of rules for abbreviated forms, but students will usually punctuate and capitalize them the way they've seen them in print, so there's no need for formal teaching, and the newer forms are often in flux anyway.[5] Instead, just explore them as an interesting aspect of language. Wikipedia and other websites have huge lists of them. Current events, geography, and the sciences are all venues for exploring these short versions of words: NAFTA and TARP, the USPS's two-letter state designations, DNA and ADHD. Kids might enjoy compiling a glossary of texting expressions. (I've been interviewed a couple of times about whether texting will destroy spelling; actually, it creates new conventions. You can text ROFL and people will know what you mean;[6] if you decide to invent TWSFIAC, no one will know you were saying "That was so funny, I almost cried.")

Where Do the Sentences Break?

Children have been told for a long time that sentences start with a capital and end with a period (or other end mark). They learn this quickly, but when they don't do it right, it's because they don't know where the sentences start and end. The traditional way to attempt to teach this is by defining a sentence as a complete thought, a subject and a predicate, and so on. Of course these don't work in practice; they make sense if you already know what a sentence is, but don't give any real guidance. Here's Merriam-Webster's definition of a sentence (from their website): "a word, clause, or phrase or a group of clauses or phrases forming a syntactic unit which expresses an assertion, a question, a command, a wish, an exclamation, or the performance of an action, that in writing usually begins with a capital letter and concludes with

---

[5] However (a rule for adults to learn), don't uppercase *fax*; it's not an acronym but short for *facsimile*. Just a pet peeve of mine.

[6] Rolling on the floor laughing.

appropriate end punctuation, and that in speaking is distinguished by characteristic patterns of stress, pitch, and pauses." This is accurate, but won't help you teach third-graders.

So what I suggest instead is a discovery lesson. An appropriate audience is children who are using capitals and periods to punctuate sentences but not consistently. (More advanced sentence punctuation appears in the next section.) Invite them to look at a couple of familiar books with a partner; nonfiction might be a good choice because it won't have the complications of dialogue punctuation. Ask them to discuss how the author knows (or decides) where the capitals and periods go; that is, where the sentences start and end. The whole class can then share their theories. Also, why do we use this punctuation in the first place, rather than writing just the words? Obviously, to ease the reader's path; technically, to mark syntactic units (but not consistently to indicate pauses, which may vary). Any answers are good; the point is to explore students' own sense of how ending punctuation works, based on their experiences with reading, because there aren't usefully teachable rules; it grows out of a sense of the language.

Next, using passages from children's books with the periods and capitals removed, invite students to figure out where the sentence breaks are. (Try to find passages without internal punctuation such as commas.) Discussion will again be a chance to explore their own sense of how the system works, and will reflect their developing knowledge. The next question is how to apply this to their own writing. Realize that the most important aspect of this lesson is to increase students' awareness of what they're already picking up from their reading, and that they still won't get it right every time. In my first book (Wilde, 1992) I told the story of Elaine, a fourth-grader who stuck periods all over the place, including before the word *I* because "periods and capitals go together." She was working out of half-baked rules that also included ideas about periods going at the end of a line, sentence, or story. She was cured through a single conference when her teacher read one of her own pieces back to her and asked her where the periods went. After that, she still had the occasional fragment error, but basically got sentence punctuation right.

Not Enough for a Sentence or Too Much: Fragments and Run-Ons

Much of what's perceived as grammar error in older students' writing has to do with more complicated sentence punctuation, and much of that has to do with fragments and various types of run-on sentences. Let's define these. A fragment is a group of words that doesn't stand on its own as a sentence; they're rarely written in a vacuum but are related to the sentences around them, as these examples illustrate:

(a) I saw a great movie. About Harry Potter.

(b) Harry Potter is amazing. Because he has magical powers.

(c) I really liked that movie. Seriously.

You can see that each of these examples punctuates as a sentence one or more words (a phrase, a clause, and an adverb respectively) that could have been attached to the original sentence. Why the fragments? For emphasis, or out of an implicit knowledge of syntax: the punctuation reflects possible intonations that the writer could have used when speaking. It would be very unlikely, for instance, to see the following: "Harry Potter is amazing because he. Has magical powers." In fact, the three examples above would all be reasonable to find in less formal writing, where sentence fragments can be a stylistic choice.

Where should teaching come in, then? You can take samples of fragments from student writing, repunctuate them, and then ask kids to compare both versions. One useful way to talk about the difference is by saying that when a piece that can't stand on its own is broken off and punctuated as a sentence, it can be seen as incorrect, but that writers will sometimes choose to do so for effect. I quickly found an example in the *New York Times*. The columnist Maureen Dowd (2011),[7] writing about *The Twilight Zone*, followed a long, complex sentence with a parenthetical fragment: "Given the

---

[7] I knew I'd be more likely to find a fragment in the less formal medium of an op-ed column than in a news story.

way Serling treated time travel, space odysseys, robots and aliens, the 21st-century technology giants would probably have been ominous in one narrative and benign in another. (Just like in life.)" A group of secondary teachers once told me that they thought it would be better for students to just be told that fragments are always wrong, but this would be bogus and limiting. It's much better to realize that there are grammatical conventions, but that this one isn't ironclad. The trick is to know what you're doing with fragments, and for teachers to help students deal with them as they come up in their writing, not through a series of rules and exercises.

What about run-ons? Basically, run-on sentences return us to the problem of not knowing where to break sentences. The following isn't a run-on sentence: "I got up and went over to my friend's house and we watched TV and then we went outside and played with the dog and when it started raining we went inside again and had some pizza and then it was seven o'clock so I had to go home so I went home." It's just a badly written, overlong sentence. The following *is* run-on: "I watched TV I went home." With a comma in the middle, it would be one subcategory of run-on sentence, a comma splice. But sometimes comma splices are okay if the clauses are short enough: "I came, I saw, I conquered." It comes down to a question of making students more aware of sentence punctuation and gradually becoming better at it as they gain more experience with written language through reading. As with fragments, use literature and their own writing to work on run-ons.

> Sometimes comma splices are okay if the clauses are short enough: "I came, I saw, I conquered."

The larger issue here, however, when we talk about "poor grammar" at the level of writing mechanics, has to do with students' writing like they talk, or just not writing very well. When I Googled "grammar lessons," my first hit was dailygrammar.com, where I found 440 lessons and 88 quizzes on parts of speech, sentence construction, and mechanics. The *Daily Oral Language* program, published by Great Source, offers two sentences a day for students to proofread and includes the following as a (weird) sample sentence to be corrected in eighth grade: "Mr. Wongs students studying the Amazon River, therefore, their teacher made a special request." I believe teachers seek out such programs because of concerns about their students' writing, but these programs won't provide a fix. I do recommend Edgar Schuster's *Breaking the Rules* (2003) and all of Constance Weaver's books on grammar (1996, 1998, 2006, 2008) for those wanting to do more work on fine-tuning the grammatical details of students' written language, particularly as part of a writers' workshop, but if their writing is weak generally it'll take time.

Formal lessons about types of sentences, such as compound and complex, just won't do it. Why would they? I wouldn't be afraid of using the terminology, but only if there's a real reason for it, related to reading or writing. You'll be boring students, wasting time, and still tearing your hair out over fragments and run-ons. There's no real shortcut around students' doing a lot of reading and writing of increasingly complex text, as discussed in Chapter 4. Students can cram rules like those for apostrophes for a test, but sentence structure and punctuation are more subtle. A dictionary can't tell you how to construct and punctuate a specific sentence.

In grades 6–8 particularly, as your expectations for students increase, focusing lessons and writing conferences throughout the year on the fragments and run-ons that your students are actually writing will be your most powerful tool for dealing with this core element of sentence mechanics.

Paragraphing

Moving up beyond the single-sentence level, traditional paragraphing instruction focuses on writing a topic sentence and then detail sentences, building from the ground up. But this formulaic approach isn't what writers really do in practice. One can take this approach if necessary, and it probably doesn't hurt to know how to do it when writing to a prompt on a test, but it doesn't make for good writing. I'm including a lesson on paragraphing here because it's an element of mechanics that operates at the discourse level, beyond the sentence, and is easy to teach and worth learning how to do well.

One of my pet peeves on the Internet, especially email and message boards, is that people write long stretches with no paragraphing. I find myself writing long paragraphs too, since I don't plan out topic sentences and detail sentences. (Does anyone?) The first three paragraphs of this chapter, for instance, were originally one paragraph. Then in reading back, I noticed how long it was, and just found logical spots to break it up. It's that simple. We can help students learn to do the same thing in a simple lesson where they look at paragraph breaks in books (or try paragraphing text that you've run together) and have a discussion about how paragraphing is a courtesy to the reader, as it breaks up big blocks of type in logical ways. Also, writers can choose to have paragraphs that are short (as in many thrillers or in journalism), long, or varied. It can then become a feature to be aware of when writing, revising, and proofreading, where it logically fits, rather than preceding the writing. In dialogue, there are special conventions for paragraphing, usually when the speaker changes. These are easy to look up and learn; students can also use a reference manual for getting them right when proofreading.

Text Features Beyond the Paragraph

Another piece of mechanics that goes beyond the mechanical is other kinds of text features, which indicate discourse levels higher than the paragraph and information outside the discourse itself. We teach them as part of reading strategies, but perhaps don't do enough with having students learn how to write them. I'm speaking of headings (including chapter headings), tables of contents, indexes, glossaries, and so on. These are especially valuable as students write informational text, an important aspect of the Common Core State Standards. As students expand their nonfiction writing through the grades and write longer pieces, they can be helped to learn about how to frame their writing for the reader through these organizational features.[8] Even third grade isn't too young to write informational chapter books, with all the organizational bells and whistles that published books offer. Helping students to develop their writing in this way approaches the whole idea of mechanics at a sophisticated level; that is, we're helping students to acquire

---

[8] Also, in writing longer fiction, give the chapters titles, or just number them? It's fun to see real authors' choices here.

tools as tiny as apostrophes and as big as chapter organization to communicate well with their readers. As you explore reading and writing nonfiction generally, think about all these text features as ways to integrate learning about high-level mechanics into students' competence in this genre. I'll finish this chapter now with some etceteras, a few other aspects of mechanics that are worth teaching and learning.

Bibliographic Citation

Anyone who's been to college is familiar with learning how to cite your sources and create a bibliography—and with professors who nitpick over them. Any copy editor with a publisher or professional journal knows that it's hard for even experienced authors to get all the details of citations correct.[9] When writing for publication, this stuff really, really matters. It's important to have all the information correct, so that a reader can find your sources, and to use a standard format because the information is so complicated and varied that it would be a mess otherwise. So why not start young, when children are writing informational text for which they've drawn information from outside sources? Even third-graders can learn to cite and create a bibliography using a simple style guide. I've created one as Appendix C, which you can add to as needed. It includes examples of the sources they're most likely to use: books, Internet, and personal communication (such as interviews with family members).

I believe that the great value of this is that students will learn not only the mechanical conventions of citation but the intellectual process of attribution when you're writing informational text for which the information came from outside your own head. As part of the writing process, this can involve learning about when to use a direct quote, as well as when and how to acknowledge your sources even if you're not quoting them. It will also help students as readers who are judging the authenticity and authoritativeness of books, websites, and other sources.

[9] I once came across a published article that cited *Teaching*, by S. A. Warner. Unfortunately, it should have been *Teacher*, by S. Ashton-Warner, so it wasn't even in the right place alphabetically in the reference list.

This 'n' That

Lucy Calkins (1980) discovered in her early work with Donald Graves that children who are actively writing learn a lot about punctuation marks as they discover a need for them as tools of meaning creation. Janet Angelillo (2002) explored the use of mentor texts as guides for teaching punctuation. I'd like to finish this discussion of mechanics with some odds and ends of punctuation marks and how to teach them as simply and meaningfully as possible.

QUOTATION MARKS: Use play scripts to show how to go back and forth between two conventions of how to write dialogue:

> JANE (screaming): I hate you.

> "I hate you," screamed Jane.

Quotation marks are highly rule-governed and therefore easy to learn to use. All the examples you need are right there in children's books. *The Day Jimmy's Boa Ate the Wash* and its sequels (Noble, 1992; the first one is also available in Spanish) are told entirely in dialogue, with no dialogue carriers. *Yo, Jo!* (Isadora, 2007) has pages where dialogue is punctuated conventionally and others where short exclamations are the only text, without quotation marks but distinguished by color and font. Graphic novels, of course, represent dialogue with speech balloons. These conventions and variations can be learned in fun ways without belaboring them.

OTHER PUNCTUATION MARKS: Wikipedia only lists 16 punctuation marks, a few of them unfamiliar, plus typographic symbols, some common, some less so. Some are appropriate for students to learn about as their writing matures, such as the semicolon; others are useful editing tools, such as the caret (particularly when writing by hand rather than keyboard); some are useful online (@), and others are fun to learn about as part of general knowledge, such as currency symbols (€ and £) and the copyright symbol (©). These conventions aren't worth spending a lot of time on but are interesting to talk about if they come up or as part of a study of language generally. Ellipses, for instance, are useful when writing in the horror genre (*The door creaked open and we saw . . .*).

FONTS: The book *Just My Type* (Garfield, 2011) is a surprisingly interesting cultural history and exploration of fonts, the actual forms and shapes of letters and other symbols. Digital publishing and font creation have created an explosion of font possibilities that kids might be interested in exploring. I'll return to this topic in Chapter 6, as part of an exploration of the alphabet, but think of the value of fonts as a writing tool. The shapes of the letters have to stay within bounds of convention, but there are phenomenal ways of working within that framework. The Museum of Modern Art in New York just acquired 23 digital typefaces for its design collection (www.moma.org/explore/ inside_out/2011/01/24/digital-fonts-23-new-faces-in-moma-s-collection/), some very clear, some sort of weird (see especially Beowolf, where a letter gets fuzzier every time it appears; you can see how it works online). Children's book designers are among those taking advantage of this new typography (Scieszka, 1998). Children themselves can take advantage of font design as a piece of writing mechanics, both inventing fonts—especially for special effects—when they write by hand, and taking advantage of fonts in word-processing programs and on the Web when writing digitally. You can, for instance, go to fonts.com, enter a search term such as "handwriting" or "typewriter," and then type in a text of your choice and see it displayed in multiple fonts. (It's especially fun with your name, and check out "School Script Lined.")

I began this chapter by looking at fussy examples of mechanical correctness such as capitalization, but have ended it with a look at the very lively topic of fonts. Students need to learn about these minor aspects of writing, which can seem tedious compared to the more exciting process of expressing your ideas and knowledge. But they're worth learning about so that writers can get them under their belts at a relatively young age and then use them automatically without worrying about them, but also use them to make creative and intellectual choices.

I'd like to just add a very brief comment on why to avoid the many detailed lessons and lengthy curricula available on the Internet and in teacher stores. I'm using writing mechanics as an example, but these lessons and curricula cover the whole range of language topics. Typically, they take every possible topic that could appear in a grammar handbook that you might use for reference and turn it into a didactic lesson, worksheets, and tests. Some of it is so basic that if teaching is needed at all, it can be done interactively and briefly. Some of it is so rarely needed that it can be looked up when necessary. This was the beginning of the first page I found when Googling "possessive nouns":

> A possessive noun is a noun that names who or what has something./ Add an apostrophe and *s* (*'s*) to form the possessive of most singular nouns./Add an apostrophe (') to form the possessive of plural nouns that end with *s*./Add an apostrophe and *s* (*'s*) to form the possessive of plural nouns that do not end with *s*.

This was followed by a 16-item test.

This is accurate, but it uses 60 very densely written words to lay out what you could do far more effectively with an interactive lesson or conference with students, a longer lesson for students who are new to possessive apostrophes, or a clarifying lesson for older students who are making the occasional mistake with them. Realize, too, that published grammar curricula for children are likely to have a topic like this for every day of the school year. I talk to teachers who say that their schools are wanting to begin teaching grammar again and therefore buy and require these programs, but they're just poor pedagogy—unnecessary, confusing, or both.

CHAPTER

3

Nitty-Gritty Grammar

Words, Tenses, Sentences, and Complexity

When people say "They don't teach grammar anymore," they're often talking about the lack of traditional topics about parts of speech, subjects and predicates, compound and complex sentences, diagramming, and so on. (Traditionalists may say that lack of this knowledge is why kids "can't write" today.) Well, here we are devoting a chapter to it, but I'm going to approach it from a somewhat different direction. Grammar in this sense primarily refers to the study of syntax, which is how words are put together in sentences (a slight oversimplification, but good enough for our purposes). In linguistics, it's one of the three major fields of scientific study of language, the other two being about the sounds of language (phonetics and phonemics) and its meaning (semantics).[1] You may also recognize these as the three cueing systems of literacy (Goodman & Wilde, 1992), where we talk about the graphophonic system rather than the phonetic and phonemic in order to take written symbols into account as well.

Neither children nor their teachers are linguistic scientists. So why should we study this topic at all? Here are the four reasons I think are most legitimate. First, it's interesting (when done correctly). Language is an impor-

---

[1] There are also other branches of study such as pragmatics, psycholinguistics, sociolinguistics, historical linguistics, and so on, but the three I mentioned are primary.

tant aspect of human nature and activity, and worthy of study in its own right. Language is also what English language arts teachers are working to help children develop their competence in, and a more complex knowledge of this largely unconscious human ability can help students become more interested in using it with sophistication. Second, having a vocabulary for talking about grammar and syntax gives us one more tool for talking about reading and writing. (For a huge, categorized list of grammar terminology that includes brief definitions take a look at www.usingenglish.com/glossary.html.) Third is that grammar content is included in the Common Core State Standards and is therefore likely to appear on tests that students are required to take. Whether we like the standards or not, we need to deal with them. Fourth, learning how grammar works can help to understand the variations that different speakers use, as I'll explore in later chapters.

There are a lot of cases made for teaching traditional grammar, but they don't hold up. (Examples of traditional grammar are exercises on identifying parts of speech, labeling compound and complex sentences, and identifying verb tenses by name.) It doesn't improve students' writing (Elley et al., 1975), and claims that it improves habits of mind were never more than wishful thinking. I'll talk at different points about specific drawbacks of traditional teaching, in many cases because it's not accurate linguistically, but want to mainly focus on how to teach grammar in intellectually sound, useful, meaningful ways.

I'd like to share one cautionary story. A student of mine, Jai In, who's an ESL teacher, recently wrote and said that her school was trying to add more grammar teaching. She wrote

> Just yesterday, I watched as a teacher attempted to teach adjectives, nouns, and verbs—all at once—cold, to a class of 29 ELLs. It was an engaging enough activity in that students were sorting words into columns, but how practical and effective?—only time can tell! Her reasoning was, "The kids have no sense of grammar: they don't know what nouns are!" I'm thinking, they do—they just don't know that what they know [how to use] as nouns are called nouns. Anyway, I'm of the thought that students should not be held back from learning about language explicitly, but in what ways can we

do it in a discovery/exploratory way, and not in a "Watch me as I show you my neat chart, not meaningful to your real life" way?

No criticism of the teacher that Jai In observed here; she meant well and assumed she was following good practice. Unfortunately, however, it's not linguistically accurate, let alone useful. One example: *green* has been both a noun and an adjective for a long time, and now it's a verb as well, an omnipresent one in fact. (A quick Google search turned up headings like "how to green your vacation" and "8 ways to green your garden.") Words can't be reliably classified as a single part of speech based on their meaning ("person, place, or thing," for instance); the part of speech is determined by the role a word plays in a sentence. Also, of course, everyone who speaks a language knows how to use nouns; but should kids be able to talk about nouns, and if so, why, and how should the teacher help this happen? That, and related topics, are what this chapter is all about.

I'm going to start at the word level, with ideas for helping children learn about parts of speech in interesting and useful ways, which should also provide them with the vocabulary they need for answering test items about them. Second, we'll explore the very geeky topic of verb tenses, thinking about how they really work in English. I've found this topic to be very illuminating for both teachers and, in a simplified way, for children. Third, we'll look at tree diagrams, a view of how sentences are put together that's much more accurate than sentence diagramming. Finally, we'll look at text complexity, how to understand and create sophisticated sentence structure. Thus we'll be moving from words, to the multiple forms that verbs take on (the only part of speech that really does so), to sentences in general, to complex sentences.

Parts of Speech

Quick, name the parts of speech! If you go to Wikipedia (not always a reliable source but useful here as a general indication of cultural knowledge), you'll find this list: noun, verb, adjective, adverb, pronoun, preposition, conjunction, and interjection. These are pretty familiar to anyone who's been in an English class.

These are the only items in the CCSS that ask students to use the terminology:

Third grade: "Explain the function of nouns, pronouns, verbs, adjectives, and adverbs in general and their functions in particular sentences."

Fifth grade: "Explain the function of conjunctions, prepositions, and interjections in general and their function in particular sentences."

A Google search for sample test items on parts of speech turned up, as expected, primarily items about identifying words in sentences as particular parts of speech. New York State's English Language Arts test for fifth grade, on the other hand, had no items on parts of speech.

But let's think about what we're trying to do here. A reasonable goal for learning about parts of speech is for students to have some vocabulary for talking about writing, and for us to feel that we're meeting the reasonable enough Common Core State Standards in this area so that students won't blow test items on the topic. Teachers will typically make comments like, "I want to be able to talk to them about using good adjectives in their writing." Well, that's not so hard, is it? The traditional list of parts of speech is just eight vocabulary words. (Wikipedia's list is fine for anyone other than a linguist.) Introducing eight new words in a science unit on the solar system wouldn't faze us at all, and these shouldn't either. (Imagine doing dozens of worksheets through the whole school year just to learn words like *orbit* and *satellite*. We shouldn't be doing it for *preposition* and *conjunction* either.)

> The traditional list of parts of speech is just eight vocabulary words. (Wikipedia's list is fine for anyone other than a linguist.)

I have a two-part plan for you: First, think about some lessons that will focus on enriching students' writing by drawing their attention to different parts of speech. Then, provide some children's books that deal with parts of speech. I'm going to describe a few lessons in detail; you could then adapt any of them to another part of speech. The first one involves adding words to your own sentence, the second one filling in words that have been removed from another author's sentences.

What Are Adjectives?

The first idea is a very basic, easy-to-plan-and-carry-out writing lesson. I invited a fifth-grader to come up with a sentence for a story. His example was along the lines of "The superhero attacked the villain with his sword." (This is a good one for this lesson because it contains three modifiable nouns.) I then invited him and other students to generate several words that could precede and describe *superhero, villain*, and *sword*. You can predict the results; they came up with a long, lively list. The next step was for the first student to pick a word or two to modify each noun and then read the whole sentence. All the students were of course impressed by how much richer the sentence was with the addition of adjectives ("The fierce, brave superhero attacked the violent, terrified villain with his sharp silver sword."), and we had a brief discussion about how they could use this idea in their writing. It was only at that point that I introduced the term *adjective*, in an off-handed way. ("See if you notice adjectives like these words when you're reading, too.") An adjective, by the way, is, roughly, a word that can fit in to the blank in this sentence: "I read a _____ book."[2] (It doesn't have to make sense; "an unkempt book" would still be grammatical.)

A follow-up conversation the next day could be a chance to talk about whether they'd been noticing and using adjectives more, and could even include the question, "If you wanted to tell someone what an adjective is, how would you describe it?" From that point on, you can just treat *adjective* like any other word the class knows, just as we understand and use most words without being able to recite formal definitions of them.

What about the other parts of speech? Three others are similarly useful for talking about writing: the verb, noun, and adverb. You could actually do

---

2 ⊢ By the way, you may recognize the *New York Times*' representation of a recent play title, *The _____ With the Hat* as containing a similar sentence slot that can highlight what a noun is. One of the play's stars, Chris Rock, mentioned in an interview that he told his children the play's name was *The Man with the Hat.*

pretty much the same lesson for each of them as I just described for adjectives. (With nouns and verbs, you'd look for synonyms or other alternatives to the word the student originally used rather than adding them to a sentence that didn't have any.) But here's my second lesson idea, presented in great detail so that you can pick and choose from different aspects to focus on.

What Are Verbs?

Below is a passage from *The Wonderful Wizard of Oz* (chosen because it's not under copyright; the questions would work with any book[3]) with most verbs, except for *be*, removed:

> "It's a mystery," _____ the Lion. "I _____ I was born that way. All the other animals in the forest naturally _____ me to be brave, for the Lion is everywhere thought to be the King of Beasts. I _____ that if I _____ very loudly, every living thing was frightened and _____ out of my way. Whenever I've _____ a man, I've been awfully scared; but I just _____ at him, and he has always _____ away as fast as he could go. If the elephants and the tigers and the bears had ever tried to _____ me, I should have _____ myself—I'm such a coward; but just as soon as they hear me _____ they all try to _____ away from me, and of course I let them _____.

(The verbs, in order, are *replied, suppose, expect, learned, roared, got, met, roared, run, fight, run, roar, get, go.*)

This is what you may already know as a cloze passage, one in which selected words are removed and the reader is invited to fill in the blanks. (The same principle is used in MadLibs®.) The first step in working with the passage is to have the class fill in the blanks with words that they think would fit, realizing that there are no single right answers. Working as a group would be a good approach the first time you do this. Take plenty of time. You could start, for instance, by coming up with as many choices as possible for the dialogue-carrier verb in the first sentence. Sentences with more than one

---

[3] A good choice for this exercise should be age-appropriate in content and relatively easy for your students to read.

verb missing are harder, so you could start with examples where only one verb is removed. Also, it's important to use a whole passage, not isolated sentences, so that you can build up a full sense of meaning and style.

Then the questions that you pose to them, continuing as partners or in a group, could be chosen from the following. I've arranged them in a progression, but these are examples from which you could pull out one idea to focus on for a single lesson. The main goal is to help students think about picking words that express the writer's meaning and have a good effect on the reader.

1. What was completing this like? Were some blanks easier to fill than others?

2. How did you know what kinds of words to use?

3. Did you try to pick words that were interesting, or ordinary, or just anything that would fit?

4. When I put in these blanks, I picked words to remove that were similar in some way. Do you have any thoughts about what the words that go in the blanks have in common? [An idea to bring out and develop is that they're all words about somebody doing something, sometimes really active like fighting and roaring, sometimes mental like supposing or expecting. Of course use the kids' word choices rather than the author's, since they haven't yet seen the latter.]

5. When you're writing, do you think much about picking just the right word, or do you just use words that fit and make sense? Let's compare the words that different class members used in these blank spaces. Do you like some better than others?

6. Let's look now at the verbs that the author, L. Frank Baum, had in the blanks originally. [Note how I just slipped in the term *verb* for the first time in the lesson.] What do you think of his compared to yours? [What I find interesting is that Baum's verbs are mostly pretty prosaic. It's a good example of how professional authors are likely to use plain language rather than overwrite.] The words he chose are fairly

simple ones; do you like it when authors write that way? When would you choose to use a more exciting verb?

7. I mentioned that all of these words are verbs. Could you talk a little with your partner about what you think verbs are? [A technical definition (the head of a clause) or a traditional one (a word that denotes an action, an occurrence, or a state of being), or a too-simple formulaic one (an action word) isn't useful here. Focus on pulling together your students' thoughts, as suggested in question #4, rather than on establishing a formal definition. All they need is a meaning for *verb* that will help them talk about verbs in their reading and writing, perhaps "a word that tells about what you're doing."]

8. [As a follow-up activity] In your reading for the next couple of days, keep an eye out for interesting verb choices that authors make. Take some notes on them if you like, and we can discuss them in a day or two.

I hope you agree with me that this is really about all that kids need to understand about verbs; that is, enough to be able to talk about them. (You could of course do pretty much the same lesson for students who already know the term.) I did a quick Google search for teaching resources on verbs, and what I found was deadly. Typical lessons defined verbs, or subcategories such as action verbs and linking verbs, very traditionally, and then provided sentences to identify the verbs in. This really seems quite pointless: not interesting in its own right, and with no connection to how you might use knowledge of what a verb is.

I'd like to make one other comment about focusing on particular parts of speech in order to improve writing. It's a common classroom activity to invite students to think of alternatives to *said* to frame dialogue: " 'Get over here,' he whispered, she screamed, they chortled," and so on. Several years ago, in a *New York Times* series, "Writers on Writing," the superb crime novelist Elmore Leonard provided ten rules for writers. Here's his third one:

Never use a verb other than "said" to carry dialogue.

The line of dialogue belongs to the character; the verb is the writer sticking his nose in. But *said* is far less intrusive than *grumbled, gasped, cautioned, lied.* I once noticed Mary McCarthy ending a line of dialogue with "she asseverated," and had to stop reading to get the dictionary. (Leonard, 2001)

Well, he has a point, doesn't he? (I'd recommend his entire list of rules.)

What about pronouns, prepositions, conjunctions, and interjections? What's to learn? Kids already use them in their speech. English language learners will acquire them as they become more proficient. They're all basically grammatical function words rather than words that carry the bulk of meaning. I sometimes think that *interjection* is on the list mainly to make sure that every possible word in a text could be labeled with its part of speech in a worksheet. I'll talk a little about pronouns in Chapter 4, and I think that middle school teachers could do some good writing lessons on choosing appropriate conjunctions (Hint: Use mentor texts), but other than that, let's move to Part 2 of my parts-of-speech plan: children's books.

I have three examples for you, with full references in Appendix D, each of them a series of books. The first and best-known ones are the late Ruth Heller's *World of Language* series, picture books for the parts of speech plus a few related topics. They're all in print, under ten dollars each, and beautifully illustrated, with rhyming text. The texts are a little heavy-handed and traditional for my taste, but they provide a quick overview of the terminology and are sufficient for feeling that you've done your job in making kids aware of the parts of speech. Brian Cleary has a similar, more recent series, *Words Are Categorical,* with less distinguished but still lively illustrations and more approachable text. His series also includes books on topics like contractions and antonyms. Michael Dahl has a series of books, *If You Were a Verb* (2006) and three others, plus an omnibus book, *Word Fun* (2008), that includes all eight parts of speech. The text isn't too elaborate and the illustrations are very contemporary. Libraries are likely to have many of the books in all three series, and they'd be a great addition to a school library. I wouldn't suggest spending a lot of time with them unless students are really interested, but students in elementary grades could be asked to read all of those in one se-ries (they're quick reads) and talk or write about what they learned. This would ensure that the students meet the grade-level standards. These books are too simple for most middle school students, who can be referred to an age-appropriate usage manual instead. (See Appendix D.)

I'd like to say a little bit about linguistic and grammar terminology be-yond the eight names for parts of speech. Is there any other grammatical ter-minology that would be useful for students to know? There's a lot of it out there. Just to take words starting with *p*, we have *particle, participle, passive, person, phrase, possessive*, and *predicate*. I'm certainly not suggesting avoid-ing these terms if you have a reason to talk about them, but would you teach them? I think a good rule of thumb is that if you have a reason to use gram-matical terminology in talking about writing, do so, but only as needed, with-out any attempt at a formal definition. For instance, "I've noticed you kids have trouble knowing how to use apostrophes with possessives. Let's spend some time exploring it." But would there ever be a need to talk about the dif-ference between transitive and intransitive verbs?

This is where the Common Core State Standards can cause a problem, I believe, at least in middle school. From the eighth-grade language stan-dards: "Explain the function of verbals (gerunds, participles, infinitives) in general and their function in particular sentences; Form and use verbs in the . . . subjunctive mood." I have no idea why these are in the standards. We all use gerunds ("Smoking is bad for you"), but I had to look up *gerund* to refresh my memory of what one is. Asking 13-year-olds to explain its function makes no sense. As for the subjunctive, it barely exists in English and its use is fading away. An example is a jocular lament my mother used to utter when she was tired of housework, with the subjunctive word itali-cized: "Oh dear, bread and beer/If I *were* single, I wouldn't be here." Or actu-ally, she probably said, "If I *was* single"; the subjunctive was dying even decades ago. The CCSS are, I believe, misguided here, and I can't in good conscience suggest how to teach to these two. Spending time on useless dis-tinctions would take away time from other, meaningful teaching that would truly make a difference to students' literacy. (Appendix B has a fuller discussion of what's more and less useful in the CCSS, and how to deal with items that seem inappropriate.)

Verb Tenses

Do you know how many tenses verbs have in English? Most people know past, present, and future, and think they should know something about tenses whose names include words like perfect and progressive, but don't really remember what they are. Yet in everyday language we use many forms of verbs. Here are 16 variations on a sentence with the verb in 16 different forms.[4] I used the uncontracted forms of the verb, but in normal speech we'd contract auxiliaries like *will*, *have*, and *am*, which I've indicated parenthetically.

1. I eat the orange.
2. I ate the carrot.
3. I will (I'll) eat the peach.
4. I would (I'd) eat the broccoli.
5. I have (I've) eaten the plums.[5]
6. I had (I'd) eaten the spinach.
7. I will have eaten the grapes.
8. I would have eaten the cauliflower.
9. I am (I'm) eating the apple.
10. I was eating the turnip.
11. I will (I'll) be eating the pear.

---

[4] A linguistic discussion of tense is somewhat different from what I'm doing here, and would have to include terminology like *aspect* and *mood* (Huddleston & Pullum, 2002, p. 116). My intent is to explore some features of verbs in English without getting too technical.

[5] Did you catch the allusion to a poem by William Carlos Williams? Check it out at www.americanpoems.com/poets/williams/1047.

12. I would (I'd) be eating the rutabaga.

13. I have (I've) been eating the cantaloupe.

14. I had (I'd) been eating the cabbage.

15. I will have (will've) been eating the raspberries.

16. I would have (would've, woulda) been eating the corn.

I'd like to take you through a guided discovery exercise with these verb forms, in order to develop your own understanding of them, and then talk about what this means for exploring them with children, including some examples of how I did so myself, as well as some thoughts about whether and why you'd want to teach kids about them at all.

Let's begin by exploring how the English tense system really works. We won't even talk about terminology at first, just look at the sentences. First, do you recognize that these forms are all part of normal speech that we, and our students, use and understand every day? Many of them will likely appear as part of longer sentences ("I would've been eating the corn all night if they hadn't shown up with ice cream."), but all of them are very ordinary.

Second, do you recognize that they are indeed different tenses, or something like that, even if you can't name them? Another way of putting it is that they differ in *when* the action occurs, even though it's hard to describe exactly how. I think we can also recognize that these differences are basically syntactic, since tense is a syntactic feature, different from the meaning changes that occur with the last word of each sentence.

Third, did you notice the relationships between them? The "bare" form of the verb, *eat*, occurs in only a few sentences. Elsewhere, it's been changed, has one or more auxiliaries added, or both. *Ate* occurs only once, and *eaten* and *eating* multiple times. We also see the auxiliaries *will*, *would*, forms of *be*, and forms of *have*, alone or in combination. So these verb forms aren't 16 unique, unconnected patterns, they're variations of a few basic elements. Can you also see a relationship between each fruit sentence and the vegetable sentence that follows it? They may not all seem to follow a pattern until I suggest applying a rule that may seem odd: consider *would* to be the past tense of *will*. This may not make sense in terms of meaning—it seems like the past tense of the future would be the present—but it works structurally. If you take the first part of the verb (i.e., the verb itself or the first auxiliary) in each odd-numbered sentence, and change it from present to past, you'll get the verb form in the even-numbered sentence that follows it.

Is a pattern starting to fall into place here? Let's put what we have into the form of a table. The sentence numbers are listed down the left-hand side. There has to be a main verb, the tense has to be either past or present, and the three other verb forms are optional.

	Tense	Will	Have	Be	Main verb
1	present				✓
2	past				✓
3	present	✓			✓
4	past	✓			✓
5	present		✓		✓
6	past		✓		✓
7	present	✓	✓		✓
8	past	✓	✓		✓
9	present			✓	✓
10	past			✓	✓
11	present	✓		✓	✓
12	past	✓		✓	✓
13	present		✓	✓	✓
14	past		✓	✓	✓
15	present	✓	✓	✓	✓
16	past	✓	✓	✓	✓

Notice that we have every possible combination of each element. Four options, yes/no choices for each, $2 \times 2 \times 2 \times 2 = 16$ verb forms. Also, the left-to-right order is fixed; we can't say "I been eating have the cantaloupe." However, if we just used each element in its "raw" form, we'd end up with sentences like "I had be eat the cabbage," which are ungrammatical; no native English speaker beyond the very youngest would say them. So how do we get to the different forms of *have*, *be*, and the main verb? The answer is a simple set of rules: *will* is always followed by the bare or unmarked version of the verb form; *have* by the past participle (*-ed* for most verbs; *be* and *eat* have the irregular participles *been* and *eaten*); and *be* by the *-ing* form. The tense applies to the first verb form (auxiliary or main verb). If you take a look back at the original sentences, you can see this process in action.

1. I eat the orange.   present
2. I ate the carrot.   past
3. I will eat the peach.   future
4. I would eat the broccoli.   conditional
5. I have eaten the plums.   present perfect
6. I had eaten the spinach.   past perfect
7. I will have eaten the grapes.   future perfect
8. I would have eaten the cauliflower.   conditional perfect
9. I am eating the apple.   present progressive
10. I was eating the turnip.   past progressive
11. I will be eating the pear.   future progressive
12. I would be eating the rutabaga   conditional progressive
13. I have been eating the cantaloupe.   present perfect progressive
14. I had been eating the cabbage.   past perfect progressive
15. I will have been eating the raspberries.   future perfect progressive
16. I would have been eating the corn.   conditional perfect progressive

What's astonishing, of course, is that you almost certainly didn't know any of this. You've been producing these 16 verb forms from a very young age, without knowing anything about how or why. Even if you at some point learned (and probably forgot) the names of many of these forms, it's very unlikely that you knew about all 16 of them.[6] By the way, if you find this boring rather than exciting, it's okay. I've gotten pretty geeky here. But this description has the virtue of showing the relationship between the tenses rather than just assigning names to them.

These verb tenses aren't unique to English. Not only do they occur in various forms in languages related to English, the linguist Derek Bickerton (2008, esp. p. 109) even discovered two creoles[7] with no historical relationship to each other (one from the interior of Suriname, South America, and the other from an island off the coast of West Central Africa) that had comparable grammatical particles (similar to verb prefixes and suffixes) that can be combined to compare roughly to some of these English verb tenses. He believes that this may be part of our genetic bioprogram for language.

Is this important background knowledge for teachers? I believe so. First, it means that we know what we're talking about when it comes to verbs rather than relying on outdated and inaccurate terminology, much of it derived inappropriately from Latin grammar.[8] Second, exploring these relationships between tenses is a lot more interesting and meaningful than just having a list of what they're called, which would be like knowing the multiplication tables just as a series of isolated facts without understanding the larger pattern that they're part of. Third, it gives us a context for understanding how these verb forms are learned. This is an important point. Using so many different forms of verbs has nothing to do with formal education and doesn't require literacy, just exposure to language. In Bickerton's view and that of others, it's part of our human heritage, just like learning to walk and having a growth spurt at puberty. We don't in any sense need to

---

[6] I've listed the names of the verb forms. Note how they correspond to the variations in the table.

[7] Languages that grew out of the mixing of parent languages, usually in colonial or oppressive settings.

[8] Latin had the following verb tenses—present, future, future perfect, imperfect, perfect, and pluperfect—for which Wikipedia displays a table for each of the mandatory endings in the first, second, and third person singular and plural, a total of 36 endings for each verb (http://en.wikipedia.org/wiki/Latin#Verbs). This terminology, with additions and combinations such as "future perfect progressive," has been cobbled onto our much simpler verb system.

learn anything formal about verb tenses in order to be able to use them appropriately.

Fourth, understanding verb tenses can inform our work with English language learners. It may take them some time to acquire the details of all of these verb forms in English (so adjust your expectations accordingly), but there's an underlying template that will facilitate their falling into place over time. Fifth, it can inform our work with different native-speaker versions of English. Not only are there variations on these sixteen forms ("I been eating the cabbage" as a variant of "I've been eating the cabbage"), there are additional ones. (See http://en.wikipedia.org/wiki/African_American_Vernacular_English for the difference between "I been bought her clothes" and "I been buyin' her clothes.")[9] Knowing the larger picture of how verb tenses work in English helps us see that these are rule-governed variations, not mistakes.

So should we talk about verb tenses with kids? (The CCSS ask only that students use them, which they do already in their speech, not explain them, though they do put them in the "conventions of *Standard* English" section, an issue we'll comment on in the discussion of usage in the next chapter; see also Appendix B.) If so, what, why, and how? Here's what I did as an experiment.

Exploring Verb Tenses

With some hesitation as to how well it would work, I carried out an exploration of these verb tenses with a class of seventh-graders; we ended up spending several 40-minute sessions on the topic. I started with just three sentences, *I walk, I walked,* and *I will walk,* and they were easily able to identify them as present, past, and future, and describe the meaning of each tense. Next, we added *I have walked* and *I am walking,* and talked in their own words about how these tenses were similar to the simple past and present, but with slightly different connotations. The students were best able to grasp all the tense variations by hearing them as part of larger sentences: *I walked home yesterday, and I have (or I've) walked home every day this month.*

---

[9] There are also variations common among most English speakers, such as the alternative future tense, "be going to," as in "I'm going to (gonna) walk."

Over multiple lessons (I saw them once a week), we kept adding more tenses. The biggest surprise to me is that they were fascinated by them. Some of the tenses seemed odd when they first heard them, but they were able to figure out that all of them had realistic meanings and were understandable given the right context, such as *I will have been walking home for a week by next Monday*. The grand finale was the week that we created all sixteen verb forms by using this formula:

Tense [past or present] (*will*) (*have* + *-en* form) (*be* + *-ing* form)[10] Verb

The way it works is that there have to be a tense and verb, *would* is treated as the past tense of *will*, and you can use anywhere from none to three of the auxiliaries. In this last lesson, I asked students to volunteer to create verb patterns until we ran out of options and had all 16. Dry? Not to these kids. When we had finished, I asked them if this was useful knowledge. They thought that not only was it interesting, it could help make them more sophisticated language users. One gave the example of sometime in the future eating dinner with her boss, and being able to say, "Normally I would have been eating [Note the past tense and all three auxiliaries] dinner with my family, but I'm lucky to be eating with you instead."

> The key to the success of these lessons . . . was taking it slow and helping students put what they were seeing in their own words and in the context of real sentences that they might use.

The key to the success of these lessons (to the point that kids were spotting me from the playground as I arrived at the school and asking if I was doing verb tenses with them again!) was taking it slow and helping students put what they were seeing in their own words and in the context of real sentences that they might use. My goals were exploratory, but looking back, I think what we accomplished was an awareness and appreciation that verbs in English are complex, but that also the students really knew how to use them. I obviously brought a lot of knowledge of linguistics to these lessons when I taught them, but the key is in starting with the language data and then just exploring it and having fun with

[10] The suffix applies to the following auxiliary or verb; more on this in a few pages.

it. I had no intention that they would remember the formula, and didn't introduce the names of the tenses, but some of them did take notes and some of them were so interested that I wouldn't be surprised if they took a linguistics class in college.

How Sentences Work

I'm going to start this section with a discussion of what not to do: diagramming and other traditional approaches to sentence study. I'll make it clear from the start that I'm not a fan of sentence diagramming; I'd like to spend a little time talking about why, as a rationale for talking to traditionalist parents or colleagues, or if you feel guilty for not doing it.

A recent book about sentence diagramming written for a popular audience, *Sister Bernadette's Barking Dog: The Quirky History and Lost Art of Diagramming Sentences* (Florey, 2006)[11] provides a lively overview and history. It's a quick read and the author has fun diagramming sentences from literature, particularly long ones. But even this author, who's written a whole book about the topic, doesn't try to make much of a case for continuing sentence diagramming as a classroom practice, and I can't either. My biggest concern with it (besides the boredom) is that it's not useful or accurate linguistically. For instance, the complex verb forms I described earlier would just be plugged into verb slots in a diagram without being analyzed, and diagrams show us nothing about the underlying relationship between, for instance, a declarative sentence and its negation (He walks; he doesn't walk). There are much more accurate and useful ways to learn about language.

Similarly, a student of mine who was doing a practicum in a high school English classroom told me that the class's entire grammar curriculum involved writing and classifying seven types of sentences, all year long. If you look on the Web for "sentence types," you can find several classification schemes, including by structure (simple, compound, complex, compound-complex), by purpose (declarative, interrogatory, imperative, exclamatory;

11- The author also wrote a book on handwriting (2009).

or statement, question, command, exclamation), or by some other set of categories. (I also found a couple of sites, intended for teachers of English language learners, that listed seven simple sentence types that really only encompassed seven types of clauses.) I remember suffering through exercises on the structural types myself. Just as we discussed for grammatical terminology in general, there's no need for students to learn about these. Everybody who knows the language produces all of these types of sentences in their speech and writing all the time, and it adds nothing to talk about them formally. I wouldn't avoid using the terminology if there's a reason for it, but I wouldn't teach it explicitly. I must admit I was quite shocked to hear of high school students spending so much time on an activity with no benefit, directed no doubt by well-intentioned teachers who felt they should "teach grammar."

The traditional argument for sentence diagramming and other traditional analyses is that they lead to better writing, but that just isn't true. Reading a lot and learning about the process of writing are what lead to better writing. I'll let the final word on this whole topic of traditional grammar come from the National Council of Teachers of English (NCTE), who issued a resolution in 1985 on this topic, which remains in place; in part, it says, "[T]he teaching of grammar in isolation does not lead to improvement in students' speaking and writing, and that in fact, it hinders development of students' oral and written language" (www.ncte.org/positions/statements/grammarexercises).

But we can still talk about how sentences are put together. What I'm going to present here is a very basic paradigm for thinking about English sentences, possibly familiar to you from an introductory linguistics class, that works by thinking about the relationship between parts of a sentence. These are most often done in the form of a tree diagram. (See Pinter, 1995, for an overview.) Think of the very simple sentence *Carmen walked.* Then consider *Exuberant Carmen walked the poodle into the Chinese restaurant.* We could analyze these sentences by diagramming them, but let's synthesize them (i.e., construct them from a formula, a list of rules) instead, and see if you agree with me that this helps us look at them more deeply. Let's start by saying that we're going to have a sentence.

Building Sentences Using Tree Diagrams

So what's a sentence? Let's create,[12] for the purposes of discussion, a rule that says a sentence consists of a noun phrase and a verb phrase, in that order. We can represent this in two ways: first, a tree diagram, which shows the hierarchical relationship between a sentence (S) on the top level and the noun phrase (NP) and verb phrase (VP) right below it:

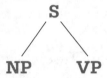

The other way to show them is through rewrite rules, in this case S → NP VP. (In both cases, the left-to-right order is obligatory.) Now we need to decide what a noun phrase and a verb phrase are made up of. Here are two very simple rules, which would account for our first sentence: NP → N and VP → V, with N and V standing for noun and verb. Well, then, what's a noun and what's a verb? We'll be choosing words from a lexicon rather than by a rule; we could make a list (*cat, dog, Carmen; run, jump, walk*), but we can also just use our commonsense understanding to come up with examples. Once we get to the names of word categories (i.e., parts of speech), we're at the bottom of our sentence-structure tree and when we fill in words we have a sentence. In this case, the tree would look like this:

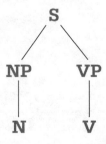

---

12 ⊢ I'm speaking metaphorically here. Actually, Noam Chomsky created all of this in 1957 and I'm just pretending that we're creating it together here.

This tree is equivalent logically to the three rewrite rules.

We then have a pattern that enables us to create an infinite number of sentences: *Carmen walked; Elephants gambol; Truth hurts.*[13] Imagine creating a very simple computer program that could use the three rules and a list of nouns and verbs (intransitive only in this case) to produce a huge number of two-word grammatical English sentences. (This is, by the way, similar to the two-word stage that children go through when they're learning to talk, though I'm not suggesting a causal connection.) I believe that even at this simple level, tree diagrams and rewrite rules are more powerful than diagramming two-word sentences (a very trivial task) because they show us that this syntactic pattern *defines* a grammatical sentence in English[14] and can *produce* such sentences.

What about our second sentence? We can actually accommodate it with just a few rule changes and additions. Let's expand our second rule, which defines a noun phrase, into NP → (Det) (Adj) N, where Det means a determiner such as *a* or *the* and Adj is an adjective. The parentheses mean that these elements are optional. Let's also expand the options for verb phrase: VP → V (N) (PP). The optional noun here, after the verb, is the object of the verb, and PP is a prepositional phrase. What's a prepositional phrase? Easy: PP → Prep NP, where Prep is a preposition. We now have a tree diagram that looks like this:

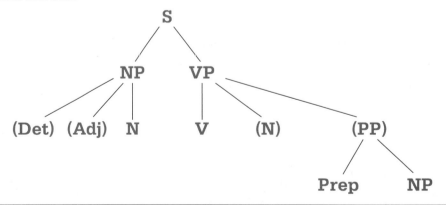

---

[13] ⊢ Infinite, or pretty much so, because language always creates new words: "IPhones ring" is a sentence that's relatively new to English.

[14] ⊢ The first rule wouldn't work for a number of languages, including Welsh, Malagasy, and Mayan languages, where the verb comes before the subject. A first rule to write for them might be S → VP NP.

What we now have is an extremely powerful sentence-generating machine, because of the optional elements. If we just go with the basic noun and verb, we have our first sentence and tons more. If we include almost all the optional elements, we get our much more elaborate second sentence, *Exuberant Carmen walked the poodle into the Chinese restaurant.*

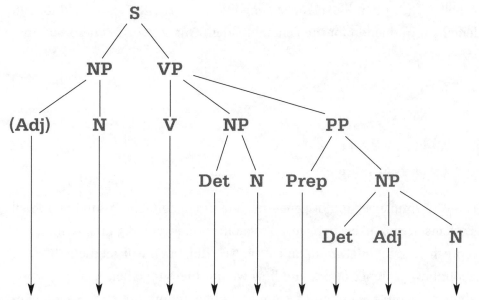

Somewhere in between, we'd get *Carmen jumped into the muddy river.*

What does this mean for you as a teacher? Imagine how much fun it would be for kids to explore all the sentences they could come up with using these tree patterns. (Remember, the number is infinite.) They could also look for sentences in literature and out in the world and see which ones fit the pattern. We haven't even gotten complicated yet—since these rules don't account for negative sentences, questions, or imperatives, or for sentences with more than one clause—but they still produce a bazillion (i.e., an infinite number of) sentences. Even so, they're just a small proportion of the larger universe of possible sentences; I was hard-pressed even to find sentences in

The Cat in the Hat that could be produced with these rules; one example that did was "Our fish shook with fear."

The great value of doing this activity would be in looking at sentences and actually seeing how they work rather than just trying to fit them into a diagram or category system. It's a thinking activity. Also, it *is* teaching grammar, but using generative grammar, which is not only more contemporary but more accurate than the traditional descriptions of English syntax that preceded it.[15] (Stephen Pinker's *The Language Instinct* [1995] is a lucid though lengthy introduction for the general reader.) Our set of rules here, summarized as

1. S → NP VP

2. NP → (Det) (Adj) N

3. VP → V (N) PP

4. PP → Prep NP

is a very simple version of generative grammar, suitable for middle school students. It's not likely to have a direct effect on improving their writing any more than traditional grammatical analysis did, but it will get them thinking about how sentences work and how we put them together. As for learning about the simple, compound, complex, and compound-complex sentences that are in the seventh-grade CCSS, we'll get to that in the next section, but let's stick with the syntax of simple sentences a bit longer.

Creating Verb Tenses with Transformations

Remember the verb tenses you just read about a few pages ago? Well, they fit in here too, with the addition of two rules: V → Tn (*will*) (*have* + *-en*) (be + *-ing*) Verb and Tn → {past, present}, with the curly brackets meaning you choose one or the other, and Verb indicating the unmarked (bare) form

---

[15] ⮑ I found a website that has a conveniently brief overview of traditional grammar for English (www.soton.ac .uk/~wpwt/notes/grammar.htm#2.4). Interestingly, it was created to help students acquire terminology for studying Old English. Its introduction includes this comment: "Since this terminology is mainly derived from Latin and Greek grammar, it isn't an ideal way of describing English, which in some respects has a very different structure."

taken from a list of verbs, or words you know to be verbs. Then here's how it works. (A little technical, but hang on for the examples.) When you're ready to go from the formula to the actual sentence, you pick a tense; any number from 0 to 3 of the optional auxiliaries; and a main verb. Then the tense applies to whatever piece comes next: If you've included *have*, the past participle[16] hops onto the next piece; if you've included *be*, the *-ing* ending hops onto the next piece.[17]

Okay, so you've chosen to go with Past (*will*) (*have* + *-en*) eat. That transforms into "would have eaten." If you've ever heard of transformational generative grammar, this is the transforming part. (The tree diagrams are the generative part.) A big shout-out to Noam Chomsky (1957), who developed it, although his work is far more complicated than these short examples suggest, and he's since moved in some different directions with his theory. Here's a tree diagram for "I would have eaten the cauliflower," and you could do one for each of our 16 sentences from the earlier section.

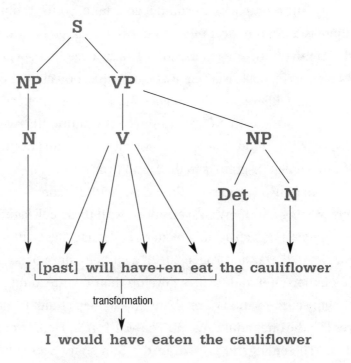

---

16 ⊢ For regular verbs, it's just the *-ed* ending.

17 ⊢ I say it hops because the technical term is *affix hopping*! (*The Concise Oxford Dictionary of Linguistics*)

Any time you have to do a morph after you've done a tree diagram, it involves a transformation, such as for negative sentences and questions. (I did not eat the orange; Did I eat the orange?) Our simplified set of phrase-structure rules (the ones with the arrows in them) only allows for a single verb per sentence; additional verbs turn up not only in compound and complex sentences (I ran out of bananas and/so I went to the bodega) but when clauses are embedded (The cat her mother had seen when she went by the pet store was really cute; three verbs). Rather than trying to classify or diagram the kinds of complex sentences we can find in our language, why not take a deeper look, through the diagrams, at the fascinating ways that even simple sentences are put together, and deal with the complex ones more directly in real reading and writing?

Sentence and Text Complexity

Text complexity isn't a simple matter, and it goes far beyond grammatical issues, but there is a grammatical piece to it. My thinking about it has been stimulated recently by two teachers. Joan Lazar, a reading specialist with middle schoolers in Teaneck, New Jersey, posed a question about how to help her students deal with really big, long, complicated sentences. Michele Hamilton and I met first on NCTE's Connected Community, where she'd posted some thoughts about the text-complexity provisions of the CCSS as they applied to her eighth-graders in the South Bronx.

I'd like to share two big ideas on the grammatical aspects of text complexity, both growing out of my conversations with these colleagues. Joan is an expert on working with struggling readers, and in fact has written a terrific book, *Now I Get It!* (Lazar and Vogel, 2010), a compendium of strategies for helping kids understand and further develop their own reading processes. We had a lengthy conversation once about how to help students make sense of sentences like the ones adults read in *The New Yorker*. Here's one sentence we looked at: "The emirs and princes of the Gulf states seemed confident that they could continue to secure their popularity with oil money, but what pressure would the spectacle of Cairo exert in Damascus, Tripoli, Rabat, and even Tehran, where a democratic movement had shown itself so vividly after the rigged ballot of 2009?" (Remnick, 2011). What a mouthful! It has 52 words, five verbs, and three major sections as signaled by commas.[18]

Although this *New Yorker* sentence is not necessarily specifically what we'd like 13-year-olds to be reading, surely they should be helped to move in this direction. There's a lot to unpack here. Background knowledge both specific (this was current events at the time it was written) and general, the context of the article it was part of, interest in the topic, and sophistication about how the world and politics work are all part of it. But as language alone, it's almost overwhelming. Certainly traditional parsing[19] or diagramming would be not only really hard but almost completely beside the point. Part of the answer is thinking about how readers can move up to the point where they can read a sentence like this (Joan's students aren't very fond of reading and haven't read much in the years before they get referred to her in middle school), and remembering that we become better readers through reading on topics we're interested in, and the more the better. (See Krashen's *Free Voluntary Reading*, 2011, where he makes the case for this eloquently and with tons of evidence.) But what about in the meantime? Joan and I agreed that kids need all kinds of support in tackling, and learning how to tackle themselves, difficult texts that they run into in their lives, and that it needs to be done through using commonsense strategies with the actual texts. No easy answers, but lots of work for teachers and kids to do together.

After Michele and I conversed online, I asked if I could visit her school, since she works just a train ride away from me, and talk to her and her students. She works with students who have followed a readers' workshop approach all through school, but she has been thinking about using more

---

[18] Thanks also to members of the CELT (Center for Expansion of Language and Thinking) email list, who responded to thoughts and questions I posted about kids' reading of passages like this. Allen Koshewa, for one, asked his fourth-grade students to paraphrase the sentence both before and after he'd explained in great detail the events it referred to. Without this background knowledge they were able to juggle the words, but their second paraphrases showed greater understanding. Interestingly, they had earlier discussed Mubarak's fall in relation to *Macbeth*, which they'd been adapting and writing lyrics for in preparation for performing a musical version.

[19] Breaking a sentence down into its parts of speech with an explanation of the form, function, and syntactical relationship of each part.

whole-class instruction of common readings and had attended a workshop on text complexity in conjunction with the rollout of the CCSS in New York. After talking to six of her students, I agreed with her that middle school is a good time to start ramping up what kids read. They were all reading a fair amount in genres they enjoyed, but they were ready to be pushed. To three young men who were interested in law enforcement, military, or firefighting as careers, I suggested that they branch out from the science fiction and fantasy genres that they enjoyed to perhaps reading memoirs about men who had the careers they were interested in. Two girls were interested in medical careers; I suggested not only memoirs but taking a look at the recent Pulitzer Prize winner *The Emperor of All Maladies* (Mukherjee, 2010), a history of cancer—not to read this entire lengthy book but perhaps to check it out from the library and try to read part of it.

When I discovered that a 14-year-old boy was interested in sports as a career but with law as a backup, I told him that in six years he might be asked to write a 15-page paper in a college history class as part of his pre-law studies. He was stunned, and thought he'd go about gaining the knowledge he needed by Googling his topic of interest (Hitler's racism) and writing down what he found there. He was further surprised when I suggested he might need to read a few books on the topic and then synthesize his ideas. We ended up with my suggestion that he could start on his path to writing that paper in six years by going to the library and asking for a young adult book on Hitler, reading it, and then perhaps writing a page or two about what he learned from it.

There are many issues wrapped up in all of this, but the major point I'd like to make is that we owe it to students — particularly children of poverty — to ensure that they're able to deal with complex language, and grammar study isn't the way to do it. They need to read a lot and they need to be helped to become better readers. We can do this in part by guiding them into gradually reading more challenging material, particularly on topics they're interested in but aren't yet reading about, and also by

> We owe it to students—particularly children of poverty—to ensure that they're able to deal with complex language, and grammar study isn't the way to do it.

teaching them how to deal with text that's hard for them. I'd like to finish this discussion by looking at text complexity in writing by some younger students, third- and fourth-graders.

These sentences come from a research study (Goodman & Wilde, 1992) of children writing in the classroom. They're part of a collection of sentences eleven words or longer that were part of our data.[20] I've chosen sentences that have three or more clauses (i.e., verbs). Spelling and punctuation have been regularized.

Third grade

But on Thanksgiving I will not eat you because I think you are nice people. [written in response to a prompt to write a letter to a turkey!]

I did not know where I was going because I did not make plans.

One day when I was at the circus a man was whipping the lions so they would jump through the circle that's on fire.

If I was a turkey I would try to run away from the people who would try to kill me for a Thanksgiving dinner.

Fourth grade

The clown helped the man get away before the horse kicked him.

When I heard he had died, I was happy because I didn't have an enemy anymore.

Little Knife got scared when his father said that he can carry the deer with him.

And the wolf screamed so loud that animals moved away so far that they never went back.

The six children whose writing we examined didn't all write sentences this complex, and none of them wrote more than several sentences like this across the dozens of writing samples we collected. But my point is that even elementary school children, even in written language, which is harder, are capable of producing fairly elaborate grammatical structures. None of these

---

[20] Technically, they're T-units (Hunt, 1965)—independent clauses and any dependent clauses connected to them. There are therefore no compound sentences in the collection.

sentences involve complex thought; they aren't particularly literary or fancy, but they reveal what children are capable of doing with language without having been taught to do so. Sometimes children, and writers generally, write long sentences that are very simple, with just a single verb. But a linguistic analysis of our eight sentences would show both independent clauses and a variety of types of subordinate ones. Where did these children learn how to produce sentences like these? From exposure to language. (Incidentally, they were Native Americans in a reservation school whose parents spoke English but whose grandparents may not have.) Our language, of course, wouldn't have complicated sentences like these if users didn't know how to produce them, but the pleasant surprise for many teachers may be that children can write them at such a young age.[21]

A related teaching idea: Have a conversation with students about why writers sometimes use short sentences and sometimes use long ones. A good way to start the discussion is to have them each look at a book they're reading and notice changes in sentence length, and invite them to speculate about the author's choices, as well as whether they notice how long the sentences are in their own writing. (It might even be fun to count words, in books and in their own writing, particularly for longer sentences.)

Sentence Expansion and Contraction

How can you get better at writing longer sentences? Here's an exercise that's been around for years: sentence expansion and contraction. Start by writing on the board a one-word sentence: "Wow." Then replace the one word with two words: "Lions roar." Then replace just one of the words with two words: "Lions eat giraffes." Then invite the students to take turns, every time picking one word of the sentence and replacing it with two, so that the sentence gets one word longer every time. What makes it fun is that you can completely change the meaning: "I rarely eat giraffes." See how long a sen-

---

[21] Children also, of course, speak in complex sentences at even younger ages. A friend's daughter, at the age of 28.5 months, said while on the way to a medical appointment, "I have to go to the doctor to see if I'm OK." This sentence contains four verbs; that is, four clauses.

tence you can create. Then if you like, reverse the process, so that your sentences get shorter every time until you're back at one word. Here's an example of an up-and-back sequence, so that you can see how it goes. (Small changes to create subject-verb agreement are allowed.)

Wow.
Lions roar.
Lions eat giraffes.
I rarely eat giraffes.
I rarely eat breakfast anymore.
I rarely eat breakfast before noon.
I rarely eat tuna salad before noon.
I rarely eat tuna salad before I swim.
The lifeguard rarely eats tuna salad before I swim.
The lifeguard rarely eats tuna with anchovies before I swim.
The lifeguard rarely eats tuna with anchovies before the children swim.
The lifeguard rarely eats tuna with anchovies before the children go diving.
The synchronized swimmers rarely eat tuna with anchovies before the children go diving.
The synchronized swimmers rarely eat tuna fish before the children go diving.
The whales rarely eat tuna fish before the children go diving.
The whales attack tuna fish before the children go diving.
The whales attack tuna fish before porpoises go diving.
The whales swallow fish before porpoises go diving.
The whales swallow fish before porpoises sleep.
Vampires swallow fish before porpoises sleep.
Vampires swallow fish before naptime.
Vampires scream before naptime.
Vampires love naptime.
Vampires bite.
Help.

My sample sentence only goes up to 13 words; groups of kids can produce longer ones. The main idea is to have fun with it (It's more fun than you'd think!), and to have experiences with the feel of longer sentences. It's an activity you can do when you have a spare moment and one that small groups or partners might enjoy doing on their own. This activity has benefits every time you do it, because it stretches writers' long-sentence-creating muscles. All of this can then lead into an ongoing discussion about how writers can vary their sentence lengths consciously as they work to create particular effects.

I'd like to mention one more thought about creating longer sentences: sentence combining. This is an activity that became popular in the 1970s and has a lot of research support (Hillocks, 1987), but has fallen out of favor, I believe largely because it can be somewhat tedious. The idea behind it is that complex sentences are created out of component parts, and that through combining components that have been pulled out from existing sentences, writers can develop a feel for coordinating ideas through the use of syntax. There are plenty of examples available on the Internet, but it's also easy to develop your own. The main benefit comes from the activity itself; you don't really need to talk about it much, other than to say it's a way to learn how to write more complicated sentences and then modeling how to do it. It's not something I'd spend much time on, but it could be done as an occasional brief whole-class activity. After students get the hang of it, they can do exercises on their own, and possibly even learn how to break down a sentence to make exercises for each other. But be warned: it's not very stimulating and is best done in small doses.

Here's how, first with a simple example. Prepare for the exercise by taking a sentence, probably a single-clause one. (*Low clouds of sunny-side-up eggs moved in.*) Break it down into separate sentences like this (it's easier to just show it than describe it):

Clouds moved in.
The clouds were low.
The clouds were made of eggs.
The eggs were sunny-side up.

Give students just the component sentences and ask them to try to combine them into one longer one. (I'd do an example first.) Working as individuals or with partners and then sharing the results works well. It doesn't matter if it ends up exactly the same as the original sentence, but you'll want to show them the original. This, like the sentence expansion and contraction activity, can be done over and over, when you have a few spare moments or a couple of times a week. A great advantage of both these activities is that they get kids to strengthen their syntactic abilities through actual experience with language, rather than talking about it. A good tone to maintain is one of playing around with sentences, making clear that this may well help them write more sophisticated sentences in their own writing. Indeed, once they're familiar with sentence expansion and combining, they can apply the techniques to revising their own writing.

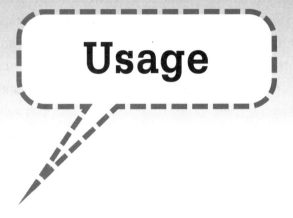

Usage

I shall talk about usage here, but you ain't going to like it. Whoa! What's wrong with that sentence? Many of you are likely to have been put off by the *shall,* the *ain't,* or both. We may think of these as grammatical errors, or oddities, but they're more accurately described as *usage* differences. Both of them sound just fine to some native speakers of English. (Alternatively, if I had written "I talk will usage about, but you not are it going to like," I would have committed actual grammatical errors, in the sense that no native or fluent speaker of English would produce them.)

Usage is perhaps the most volatile linguistics topic, especially for teachers, because people get upset and judgmental when others' usage varies from their own. At best, they think it's charming (the Southerner's *y'all*); but often they think it's a sign of ignorance (with *ain't* as a prime offender) or language decline (*whatever*). Teachers who work with children of poverty are very aware that those children's usage may hinder their ability to get ahead once they get out into the wider world. (Richer children also move into worlds beyond their own community, but we tend not to worry about their usage.)

Usage may be the most important feature of language for teachers to understand, and also the most likely to be saddled with misconceptions and prejudices. How we deal with usage will have a much greater impact on children's lives than whether they know the names of parts of speech, as it will affect not only their own speech but how they perceive and judge others'. It will affect their chances when they apply for jobs and try to fit in to social networks, and will also affect those who become the bosses and other gatekeepers.

Usage as a Social Marker

Language usage is a social phenomenon: not only is it a product of the people that you grow up around and live among, but it's mostly invisible to us unless we're talking to someone from a different group, where they "say things differently." Rules have been written to describe usage, but it comes down to whether the way someone is speaking sounds right to you. Imagine a very sheltered American who had never heard a British speaker and was dropped down in London or Liverpool one day. Speech would sound odd to her: the accents, some of the vocabulary, and some of the grammar. The same for a sheltered Londoner or Liverpudlian landing in New York or New Orleans. A time machine taking us back to Shakespeare's Stratford would have the same effect; Chaucer's England even more so. The natural human response in all these situations is to think, "They talk funny; have an accent; are saying things wrong." This is probably human nature, but it's reciprocal; the Chaucerian millers and prioresses would be saying the same thing about us.

The first part of our discussion of usage therefore needs to explore the nature of what produces the varieties in social groups that lead to language difference: time, place, social group, and context. We also need to think about the individual speaker's proficiency: whether he's a native speaker or a second language learner, and whether he's an adult, or a child whose language hasn't yet fully matured. Usage between one version of a language and another can differ in pronunciation,[1] grammatical features, and vocabulary.

---

[1] We won't try to explore larger pronunciation issues, such as an Australian accent, but will mention some examples of individual word pronunciations that can end up feeling like errors to speakers from a different group.

Let's look at a couple of examples. When you hear someone else say something that sounds odd or wrong to you, think about what you'd say instead and why it seems better to you. One that I hear mentioned a lot is *funner*: "Shopping is funner than studying." This is a grammatical difference since it has to do with how we construct the comparative forms of words; critics will usually say the usage should instead be *more fun*. Another example is the prevalence of public cursing, four-letter words in particular. These words have been part of the language for a long, long time and have been used by many speakers, particularly men. But sixty years ago it was very rare to hear them in a public place like a subway or restaurant.[2] This is a vocabulary change; the words aren't new, but the social acceptability of their use has changed. Many people, of course, still find them offensive, but the mores of using them have changed, so we have a situation where some people use language that's been around for a long time, but in a way that may feel wrong to others, particularly older people. In another sixty years, usage may have changed to the point where public cursing doesn't strike anyone as wrong. (Or not; we can't predict language change.)

> In another sixty years, usage may have changed to the point where public cursing doesn't strike anyone as wrong. (Or not; we can't predict language change.)

In talking to teachers, I suggest that when they hear a student say something that doesn't sound right to them, they think about what the likely cause of the perceived error is. Let's think first about generational changes. When you hear someone say *you guys* to a group as a plural form of *you*, how does it sound? Normal, too informal, improper? The answer is likely to depend on your generation, or more precisely which generation's language usage you feel comfortable with and use yourself. A middle-aged colleague of mine lightly reprimanded a student teacher for using the term *you guys* with children and said it sounded unprofessional.[3] Let's hold off on judgment of the usage for now, but realize that it's

---

2 ⊢ I was going to say shopping mall, but they barely existed 60 years ago, unless you lived near Seattle and went to Northgate starting in 1950.

3 ⊢ Also, some people think that it's sexist, since it uses an originally male term to include both genders.

a relatively new term in English and is more likely to be used and accepted by younger Americans. More broadly, has someone older than you criticized a use of language that sounds fine to you, or have you been bothered by a usage from someone younger than you? These generational usage changes are often developed by teenagers who then carry them into adult life; then they become part of the language as a whole. Over a long period of time, these lead to the changes that make our language different from Chaucer's, but in the short run, younger people will use language that older people don't like.

Different places also produce different usages. My sister Janet and I both grew up in Plainfield, New Jersey, but she's lived in Madison, Wisconsin, for 40 years and now refers to parking garages as ramps, as people there do. A 2002 movie set in working-class Scotland, *Sweet Sixteen*, was provided with subtitles for American viewers. Watching it, I was struck in part by the roughness of the cursing, but even more by the comment of the lead character as he watched an attractive girl pass by his window. Where an American teen might have said, "Whoa, she's hot!," this lad commented, "Is she not stunning?" which sounded quirkily formal to my ears. In the South, people say *y'all* and the Pittsburgh-area second-person plural *yinz* has become a badge of regional pride that now appears on T-shirts.[4] A lot of these regional differences, whether within the United States or from other English-speaking countries, may not strike us as errors or overly slangy the way generational differences often do.

However, some usage differences between different groups within or across regions, particularly social-class and ethnic or racial groups, tend to carry a lot of social weight, usually in the form of stigma placed on the usages of the lower-status group. When someone uses the language of her community, what we're hearing isn't an error, but it may feel like one to an outsider. Members of that community, sensing the stigma, may be critical of their own language as well. We can hear these language features in expressions such as

---

4 — Why do we need all these special second-person plurals anyway? Why don't we have a "regular" one that doesn't sound slangy? It's not that we never had one, it's that we lost the second-person singulars *thee* and *thou*; as *you* started to feel more singular, we developed new plurals. (Jochnowitz, 1983)

"I might could work" (from regional English; see www.randomhouse.com/wotd/index.pperl?date=20001120 for a discussion of it) and "He be goin' to the park" (from African American vernacular English). For now, we'll keep the focus just on realizing the origin of these various language differences. Why do people living in the same area, from the same generation, speak differently from each other? It's about who your community is. To the extent that different racial groups and different social classes lead separate lives, their language will differ, even when they're living virtually side by side. I lived for three years in a Native American First Nation community (then called a reserve) in Canada; the economic life of the people there was closely intertwined with the neighboring town, where most of their working and shopping took place, but their social lives were largely segregated. As a result, their language was different, not dramatically but to the extent that you could tell on the phone whether you were speaking to someone from the reserve or someone from town. Here are two examples of reserve speech. Where I'd say "Wow," they might say "Ho-WAH!" And if they found something sort of sleazy, they might say "Errrr," but only if they were women or girls.

Finally, usage will differ between individuals as a result of their proficiency in the language. Some usages that sound like errors may be the result of influence from the speaker's non-English first language, as when a Chinese speaker interchanges *he* and *she*. There are features of children's language that are incorrect and disappear as the speakers get older: "She walkeded." "It's mines." There's also a greater proficiency that comes with greater literacy and more extensive education; but this is likely to manifest itself primarily in a bigger vocabulary, more ability to produce formal language, and perhaps more sophisticated sentence structure. It's in large part the social opportunities that come with more education, particularly college,[5] that enable people to acquire the "mainstream" language style as an alternative to their home versions, first in speech, then carried over to writing. What's typically perceived, indeed stereotyped, as speech that contains errors because the speaker is uneducated is more likely to be just the home

---

[5] "Particularly" because K–12 American schools are highly segregated by income (Grant, 2009).

language of someone from a lower-status community. Someone with little education speaking the home language of a white middle-class community won't face that same judgment.

> What's typically perceived, indeed stereotyped, as speech that contains errors because the speaker is un-educated is more likely to be just the home language of someone from a lower-status community.

Before exploring some teaching ideas for usage, I'd like to mention that reading is the most important way for children to acquire usage patterns that aren't already part of their language, particularly the more prestigious ones (Krashen, 2004). This is in part because written language is more formal generally, but also because these forms are most efficiently acquired rather than learned; that is, picked up unconsciously rather than through teaching and formal practice.

Talking About Usage with Students

So let's explore what this means for teachers. The concept of usage is largely too abstract for younger children to understand. They're still just figuring out how to talk and can't conceptualize in any useful way the idea that some varieties of language are more "acceptable" than others. But beginning by around third grade, there are many ways we can explore usage. I'd like to make it clear that in this chapter I'll be talking primarily about oral language. Written language is a different animal, with its own expectations and conventions, one of them being a more formal register.[6]

Usage has often been taught as a matter of right and wrong, and indeed is perceived that way. Many, if not most people, say they're bothered by errors in other people's speech, even though they themselves use forms that someone older or stuffier than themselves would call mistakes. This stance towards usage is not only wrong but pointless and harmful.[7] If correction changes people's speech (which is doubtful), it's likely to be at the cost of making the speaker feel defensive, self-conscious, annoyed, inadequate, or

---

[6] Defined as a form appropriate for a particular context.

[7] I'm not talking here about real mistakes, like calling an eggplant an avocado; usage would be calling an eggplant an aubergine, as a British person does.

puzzled. If the speaker's language is that of a group that has a history of being stigmatized, these feelings are likely to be stronger, and to perhaps include anger or defiance. ("I don't want to talk White" [Ogbu, 2003].) Taking an exploratory approach will be more productive and respectful, and will involve more learning for students. The following lesson suggests a way to start. This lesson focuses on just noticing usage differences, and understanding that they come from differences in time and place.

What Is Usage?

What you want students to learn is that there are differences in the way people speak that have to do with their generation and community. If possible, think of some words or expressions you use that older people don't like, and some that your students use that you didn't at their age.

Begin by providing students with the following passage:

> I got up at half eight and took the lift down from my flat. I walked over to the high street where I stopped in a store and put some crisps and biscuits, along with some nappies for the baby, in my trolley. Walking home, I nearly got hit by a lorry at the junction, so, feeling a bit knackered, I watched football on the telly until my mum got up.[8]

Then use some of these ideas to prompt a discussion: Can you translate this? How could you find out what the words mean? Do you know who speaks this way? What do you think of talking this way? Why would people speak this way? The big ideas to help them understand is that there are differences between British and American vocabulary on a number of words, and that this is because we speak the same language but live in different countries. The languages have been growing apart since the first British settlers came here hundreds of years ago. If interested, students could research etymology and find out whether the British or American word is older in each case. For instance, *diaper*, used in America, has been around since the 14th century, while the British word *nappy* stems from 1927. (In some cases,

---

8 Britishisms from http://therussler.tripod.com/ling/british_equivalents.html#usage

both words already existed but came to take on a different meaning in one country. Other words, like *lorry* and *truck*, are currently used for things that have only existed since America was a separate country.) It isn't that one is right and one's wrong; they're just different.

Ask the students if they're aware of how some Americans speak differently from others, both within their own community and elsewhere in the country. Their knowledge of this will of course depend on their age and experiences. They'll be inclined to speak about accent at first, since this is often what stands out, but try to encourage them to think about differences in words and expressions. It should also include whether there are differences between the way they and their parents and grandparents speak. Bring in some examples of usages that they have in their language that you didn't have in your generation and some ways that you speak that your parents didn't. (This shouldn't be words for new technologies but new ways of saying things, including new uses for old words, like "I texted my friend.") The big idea from this part of the lesson is that language changes over time (from one generation to the next) and is different from place to place, even in the same country.

For follow-up you can watch a British children's movie (I'd recommend *Millions*, 2004), or an American one from several decades ago (try *Heidi*, 1937, with Shirley Temple), to see what language differences students can pick out (other than accent). Also, you could ask students to write a short article for other children their age about why people talk differently from each other.

Now that we've established this foundation, I'd like to look at a variety of specific usage questions and how to deal with them. These can be best explored first by noticing examples of what concerns or bothers you in your own students' usage, then figuring out which of four categories it falls into. We can also look at the Common Core State Standards, usage manuals, other curriculum materials, and usage guides through these lenses, and then think about *what* should be taught and *how* to teach it. I'll describe the categories and then devote a section of the chapter to each one.

First are generational changes and usages. These fall into two categories: "Kids today don't talk right" and "Nobody follows that rule anymore." Second are variations between social groups: "People who are [insert name of group] speak bad grammar." Third are usage differences commonly found in English language learners: "Kids who speak [insert language name] have trouble with [name grammatical feature]." Fourth is word choice: "People are always using [word A] when they should be using [word B]." If we can define what we're looking at in each case, we can make appropriate teaching decisions.

Generational Usage Issues: Lost Battles and Losing Battles

Do you find yourself bothered by anything about the way kids today talk? Were your parents annoyed by anything about the way you talked as a teenager? Well, you're a normal part of human history. Adults have always thought that kids were going to the dogs and that the way they talked was part of it. This was as true in 7th-century China (or wherever) as it is today. To put it in perspective, let's look at some usages that are no longer an issue.

Have you ever used the word *shall*? If you search online for lessons on using *shall* and *will*, you'll find that they're primarily designed for English language learners and say that *shall* is rarely used anymore, except in Britain, or in occasional questions using *I* or *we*, such as "Shall I help you?" Take a look at these examples of the way they were formerly used, and see if they make any sense to you:

I shall go tomorrow.

I *will* go, even if they don't want me to.

He will (he'll) go tomorrow.

He *shall* go, even if they don't want him to.

For first person (*I* or *we*), one used *shall*; the rest of the time, *will* was the correct form. With an exception: a speaker who wanted to express a sense of determination, promise, or command switched them, as in the second and fourth examples (Garner, 2009). This is the English of another era; we shall not see its like again. (And of course, especially in speech, even *will* is most often abbreviated to *'ll* and joined to the subject: "John'll go.") A couple of generations ago, adults were probably bemoaning the loss of this distinction, but we don't care, do we?

> A couple of generations ago, adults were probably bemoaning the loss of this distinction, but we don't care, do we?

The word *movie* was first used in 1911, according to Webster's. A 1912 punctuation handbook (Klein) referred to it as a word that should be put in quotation marks,[9] much as you'd do if you were writing today "That guy had 'Lego hair.'"[10] We don't just have new words, we've added new usages and dropped old ones. There are a bunch of old usage rules out there that people don't really follow, and that English teachers have a reputation of correcting but may not even really follow themselves. *Whom* is almost gone (I've had college students laugh at me for using it!), we all split infinitives with impunity, we'd be hard-pressed to explain the difference between *lie* and *lay*, and so on. The author June Casagrande has had fun on the Web (http://conjugatevisits.blogspot.com/) and writing books (2006, 2008), giving her own take on a lot of these old usage myths. Some of them are niceties that copy editors might proofread for, but there's no point in teaching them to children.

What about usages that are in transition? At the Whole Foods supermarket chain, there are check-out lines for those with "10 items or fewer," where most other stores use *less*.[11] But I'd never bother talking about this distinction with children, because it's on its way out. If you're tempted to try to enforce your own pet language peeves on your students, even though their usages

---

[9] His example and discussion: "'"Movies" showing war scenes that arouse the martial spirit are objectionable to all pacifists.' The above sentence contains two words that are treated as they are found today in practically all periodicals and books using them. The words *movies* and *pacifists* . . . are newcomers to English, and are not found in any dictionary. Why is the former put in quotation marks and the latter not? It is probably because all editors recognize 'movies' as a word of doubtful propriety" (p. 183).

[10] I found this one on urbandictionary.com and don't know if anyone's really said it!

[11] The stores also have "When you wanna bake" (*sic*) on the sign indicating the aisle where the flour and sugar are.

are becoming the norm, think about those teachers of 50 years ago who in-sisted on *shall*. Why fight a losing battle? Why should your idiosyncratic pref-erences be more valid than those of the majority of the users of English? The online magazine *Slate* recently criticized the antiquated practice of leaving two spaces after a period when typing, pointing out that teachers insist on it just because they were taught that way.

It's very important to realize that these changes aren't out of ignorance, or laziness, or anything else that should be stigmatized. They just happen to be generational changes in grammar that are actively going on right now and are therefore very salient to our ears, no different than all the other changes that have ensured that we aren't speaking Middle English anymore. So what's a teacher to do? Correct them, ignore them, talk that way yourself? (Which you probably already do, though the specifics will depend on what genera-tion you're from.) Actually, it doesn't matter. Language changes in the ways it's going to change, and teachers have never stopped it from happening. I think the best approach is to help kids learn about it. If you hear children say-ing something that grates on your ears, and it's a grammatical form that's starting to appear in society generally,[12] think about what the change is and explore it with children. But realize that today's speech is the air that they've always breathed, and they may not even be able to see the grammatical difference be-tween *funner* and *bigger*. So why annoy them by cor-recting them?

> Realize that today's speech is the air that they've always breathed, and they may not even be able to see the gram-matical difference between *funner* and *bigger*. So why annoy them by correcting them?

I'd like to just say a little about literary license too, using an example that literally came in through my window. When I lived in a ground-floor apartment with a fair amount of foot traffic outside, as I was writ-ing this section I heard a man outside call out a couple of times, "Say it loud! I'm black and I'm proud!" (from the classic James Brown song). Being in a grammar mode of thinking, I found myself wondering if it should be "Say it loudly"? Of course not! Poetry trumps grammar.

---

[12] Reality TV may be the cutting edge of changing speech forms, though when its cast members are working-class, their speech is often mocked.

I'd like to highlight a few usages that are currently in transition and are likely to be perceived as "incorrect" by many teachers even though they use them themselves; I'll begin with a lesson about *funner*.

Funner

What you want students to learn is something about what we know about how comparative adjectives are formed. This is mainly an awareness and exploration lesson, but includes this focus: Some people think the word *funner* is bad English. Why do they think so and what should you do about it?

There aren't any simple rules for how to form comparative adjectives (that is, whether to use the suffixes *-er* and *-est*, or the words *more* and *most*). You can do a Google search for "comparative forms of adjectives" and see for yourself; I'm not going to explain these complicated and boring rules here but instead present a kid-friendly lesson.

Adding inflections to *fun* grates on a lot of people's ears, but it's been around for a couple of decades now, and has been appearing in print more often. (I saw *funnest* on a billboard for the Oregon Lottery at least a decade ago.) One might ask why it should even be a problem; don't we always add *-er* and *-est* to one-syllable adjectives (*sadder, greener*) and save *more* and *most* for longer ones (*more delightful, most mournful*)? Here's why it bothers people. *Fun* has changed from being merely a noun to being an adjective as well (since around 1846), but we don't really notice it until we add the inflection. We can talk about going to a fun party, and nobody blinks, but if we say it was the funnest party ever, people may look askance. (Grammar Girl has a fairly long piece on this issue: http://grammar.quickanddirtytips.com/is-funnest-a-word.aspx.)

For this lesson, have ready a list of words whose comparative forms use the endings *-er* and *-est* and others that use *more* and *most*. Here's my list, but use your own if you like. (A box of crayons would make this even funner.)

First group:	Second group:	Possibly either group:
red	orange	purple[13]
brown	silver	
green	lavender	
yellow	magenta	
	turquoise	

Start with some other examples, ideally with some pictures that illustrate a comparative range. The more interesting the better: *This tornado is scary; that one is scarier; the other one is the scariest of all. This spider is monstrous; that one is more monstrous; the other one is the most monstrous of all.* Turn and talk: What did you notice about the two ways to compare adjectives, words that describe things?

Using your list or words that students choose themselves, invite the students to work with partners to come up with some comparisons of their own: *The sky is usually bluer than the ocean; which is more orange, a mango or a papaya?* Younger kids might want to draw pictures, older ones try to top each other in ingenuity. Raise the following question: How do you know when to put an ending on the word, and when to use *more* and *most*? The most reasonable answer: usually you use the endings on one-syllable words and *more* and *most* for longer ones, but in the end it comes down to what sounds right. How do we know which to use? Just from our experience speaking the language. If English isn't your first language, you may not get it right every time, but it's a pretty small piece of language, so not a big worry.

Next question: How do *fun/funner/funnest* fit in to this pattern? Most likely answer: they fit right in because *fun* is a one-syllable word. Given that, why do some people think they don't sound right? Ask the students if they think this pattern is one that kids are more likely to use than adults are. Why do they think that's so?

Guess what, kids? A lot of adults just don't like the way that *funner* and *funnest* sound! There isn't any reason for it, it's just something that kids say

---

13 ▷ See http://en.wikipedia.org/wiki/List_of_colors for a huge illustrated list of color names, including a link to Crayola colors—great just to look at or as a vocabulary-builder for kids.

today that grownups don't like, even though it makes perfect sense. (They may not like the music you listen to either, because it's different than what they grew up with.) But we want to be polite to adults, so if one of them tells you that these words are wrong, just smile and say "You're right, sir/ma'am, my bad." If you ever see *funner* or *funnest* on a test, realize that adults wrote the test and want you to say it's wrong.

Readers, are you shocked at the above? I believe it's the only intellectually honest and helpful way to talk about the topic. You don't want to be one of those adults who tries to make up a reason why a perfectly reasonable usage is considered wrong. Indeed, when I asked a friend of mine, a veteran teacher, to explain what the problem was, she came up with some wrong answers (e.g., "It's because of the spelling" [perhaps confusing *funner* with *funnier*]), and finally could only say "It just sounds wrong," which of course it doesn't to children. Almost certainly, in 50 years people will wonder what the fuss was about.

For assessment and follow-up, you can ask students to write something about what they know about how to compare words. To what extent is there a rule, and what should you do if you aren't sure for a particular word? Take a look at some children's books that are built around comparative adjectives. Some good examples are the Robert Wells series (see Appendix D for titles) and *Extreme Animals* (2006). This could spark some writing ideas, either as a research project using sources like *The Guinness Book of World Records* in its various formats or with children writing language-pattern picture books for those younger than themselves. Students might enjoy trying to write an op-ed piece about why the words *funner* and *funnest* should be considered acceptable usage in today's English. Two picture book resources are *If You Were a Suffix* (Aboff, 2008) and *Pig, Pigger, Piggest* (Walton, 1997).

Case Usage for Two Linked Pronouns

Next, let's look at pronoun case. I'd like to suggest that we not bother with those that have gone through a transition to the point that virtually everyone uses the new form. Most of us would be hard-pressed to remember when we'd last heard *whom*, or someone saying "It is I" rather than "It's me." Saying "To whom are you writing?" rather than "Who are you writing to?" is stuffy and artificial. When writing for publication, the older forms may still be adhered to, but they're so unnatural that most authors don't think about them, and the change is usually made by a copy editor. It's just not reasonable to expect students in elementary and middle school to be able to proofread at the level of expertise of a copy editor.

The one transitional usage that I think is worth discussing with students (because changes have occurred in oral language that are still frowned upon by many) is the use of compound pronouns with *I* and *me*. I've frequently even heard teachers use the "me and Jimmy" subject form. No native speaker would ever say "me had a good time," but when you add someone else's name to the sentence it's not as intuitive to use *I*; even more to the point, as the "me and Jimmy" form has been used more widely, it sounds more natural and its use has almost certainly accelerated. Also, more people have begun using the technically incorrect "told it to Ana and I" form, presumably because *I* just sounds more proper if you're not sure which form to use. In speech, people are going to say what they say, and these two changes are likely to be even more well established when today's students are adults. However, they're worth addressing for writing, and can be covered in a brief lesson.

> What you want students to learn is that there are ways to use *I* and *me* in writing and formal speech that are a little different from the way we tend to use them in informal speech.

What you want students to learn is that there are ways to use *I* and *me* in writing and formal speech that are a little different from the way we tend to use them in informal speech. For younger students, focus on the "me and Jimmy played" version; for older ones, maybe touch on the "told it to Ana and I" form, but only if you hear kids using it. The phrasings that are traditionally considered correct are: "Jimmy and I played" and "told it to Ana and me." The reason is obvious if you're using just the pronoun: "I played," "told it to me."[14] (These "errors" may occur with other pronouns

---

[14] It's also traditionally been explained as a matter of "politeness" to put the other person's name before your own.

as well: "Her and me played.") Centuries ago, some English nouns had different cases, but now only the pronouns do, and our sense of what sounds right is based on the language we hear around us, with the "incorrect" forms increasingly common. The old way of approaching this topic was through defining the terms *nominative*, *objective*, and *possessive* case. Don't go there!

Start off by writing matching paragraphs (or find a passage in a book and reword it) so that one version uses the "incorrect" form for pronouns in compound structures and the other uses the standard version. Have students read both versions and talk with a partner about how they sound to them. They may already realize that "Jimmy and I played" is "correct," or they may find it stuffy or confusing. The major teaching point is this: When we're talking to our friends, we're often going to say "me and Jimmy played," but when we're in a more formal situation or writing, "Jimmy and I played" is considered more proper. The problem is remembering to do it and then getting the formal version right. Here's an easy trick: Take out the other person's name and try saying it with just the *I* or *me*. You'll be able to tell. This is also a trick to use if you see this on a test.

You can follow up with a list of example sentences, some already "right" and others not, and see if students can tell which form to use. You can also invite them to keep an eye out for these compound noun/pronoun structures in their reading. I'd recommend leaving the students' informal speech alone in this matter, but bring it up if you see it in writing or in more formal oral situations such as giving a talk.

If you're concerned about students' blowing this on a standardized test, and think it's likely to come up, find or create some sample test items. (You can Google "pronoun case test items.") Here's how I'd use them: walk through several of them orally and talk about reasons why you'd make one choice over another in the formal writing context that tests assume. Then have students try a page on their own, and talk through any divergent answers. (See Taylor & Walton, 1998 for a rationale for providing a small amount of coaching to help students demonstrate their existing knowledge in testing situations.)

Other generational usage changes are primarily vocabulary choices: every generation develops new slang to recognize what's good and bad, the types of music it listens to, the technology that's come along, what it does behind its parents' backs, and so on. We'll talk about new language and how to help kids think about it in Chapter 6. I'm going to move on now to social-group differences in usage, but a few final words about generational usage issues and how to work with them: teachers who try to resist the next generations' language are like rocks in a raging river: we can't stop the flow, and when we're gone no one will remember or care about our resistance. I think our job is to delight in language's ebb and flow, while making sure that children have the language tools they need for dealing with the older generation, particularly in more formal situations. Remember, also, that someday they'll be the ones conducting the job interviews, where they'll be saying, "So you were like, the job at the children's camp was like, the funnest one you ever had?"

Social-Group Usage Issues

This is the most loaded of usage topics, since it deals with what social groups Americans are part of and what their language reveals about their group membership. In the next chapter, I'm going to talk about the larger topic of language prejudice among native speakers of English and how teachers can challenge it, but here I'll explore some particular usages that can be addressed in the classroom. These are usages found in the informal speech of many Americans, but are particularly associated with working-class speech of all races, particularly Southern, and African American speech.

The best book for educators that I've seen on the language variation among American native speakers is *Understanding English Language Variation in U.S. Schools* (Charity Hudley & Mallinson, 2011). In particular, it gives detailed analyses of features of Southern English and African American Vernacular English (AAVE), crucial reading for teachers of those groups. In this section, I'm going to focus on five features that are a small part of these speakers' English (one or both groups) but can have a disproportionate effect on how they're perceived by others, particularly employers and other gatekeepers. These are, in rough order from simplest to most complex, dropping *g*'s; two alternative past tense forms; *ain't*; double negatives; and alternative subject/verb agreement forms. (These forms are also used by some other Americans.) (Hudley and Mallinson also mention other features, such as pronouncing words like *pen* and *pin* the same and using pronoun forms like *hisself* (in Southern English), and, for AAVE, reducing consonant clusters to a single sound such as *des* for *desk* and phrasings with *it* such as "It's a pencil in the drawer." These can be approached in similar ways.

Dropping one's *g*'s is sometimes stigmatized but is also pretty widely accepted as a way of sounding a little more down-to-earth. I do it myself; even if you, the reader, don't, you must (if you listen closely) admit that many if not most educated people do, including, as mentioned earlier, at least the last three presidents, in their public if not their most formal speech.

I had a conversation recently with a student of mine, a high school teacher who admitted that he was put off by a colleague who dropped her *g*'s, because "she should know better." (This teacher is very precise in his own use of language, he believes in part because he came from a working-class background himself.) Is it clear that there's nothing wrong linguistically with this speech pattern? (Technically, it involves not even dropping a sound but changing one; the letters *ng* represent a single sound—the one heard at the end of *sing*, not a blend of two, which speakers then change to just an *n* sound.[15]) One might object that the speaker isn't pronouncing the word the way it's spelled, but we don't object to speakers' not pronouncing the silent letters in words like *knife*. Of course it's not logic that's the issue here; it's the associations that the speech pattern carries.

These social-class features of speech are often considered to be markers of education, but they're more markers of origins. Middle-class students typically don't say "he come over last night" in the first place, regardless of how few years of school they've attended. Where education comes in is that it's

---

[15] Or it involves the change of the vowel sound. In normal speech, the *-ing* suffix is often pronounced *een* rather than *ing* (see if saying "takeen" sounds as natural and "correct" to you as "taking"), so the *g*-dropper is actually just changing a long *e* to a short *i*.

supposed to help working-class students change their speech to a middle-class version. We tend to take this for granted, but think about it. Why should middle-class speech be considered the model for everyone? We'd be horrified at the idea that poorer children should be criticized if they don't wear the expensive clothing brands that the richer kids do (and in fact are bothered when children rag on one another's running shoes and hoodies); why should they have to change the way they talk?

Of course the dirty little secret behind all of this is class prejudice in American society. In many ways, looking down on those who have working-class features in their language is a form of snobbery, even if unintentional, and members of the working class absorb these attitudes as well and become self-critical.

> Of course the dirty little secret behind all of this is class prejudice in American society.

Are there any fashion choices made by social groups other than your own that grate on you? (I won't give examples for fear of offending someone.) I think we all have these reactions, but should probably feel ashamed of ourselves when we do. I'm proposing here that we should look at language in the same way. If we can get rid of our own snobbery, I believe we'll be better prepared to help our students deal with language snobbery in society. Given that context, however, we should still think about these features and how to work with them.

Droppin' *g*'s

There's a terrific children's book called *Possum Come A-Knockin'* (Van Laan, 1992) written in folksy Appalachian rhyme: *Brother was untanglin'/all the twiny line for fishin'/while Sis was tossin' Baby/and Pappy was a-whittlin'.* As you can see, not only are *g*'s dropped, but verbs may be preceded by the prefix *a-*, a feature whose origins are explored here: www.pbs.org/speak/seatosea/americanvarieties/a-prefixing/background/. Reading the book aloud can be an occasion to talk about the style it's written in; you can invite students to share their thoughts about how it's different from the everyday speech of most Americans and the effect that it creates. Then, for contrast, read part of it aloud again using "regular" verb forms, such as *knocking* rather than *a-knockin'*. How does this change the whole tone of the book? Why did the author choose to use the language that Van Laan did?

For another contrast, try reading this passage (or one from a children's book) aloud, first as written and then with dropped *g*'s:

> I was living in Tucson when I first discovered ice-skating. Going to the rink with a few of my friends soon became my favorite way of spending a Saturday afternoon. At first I was slipping, sliding, and falling all the time, but then I got better at it and was gliding along, spinning, and twirling like an Olympic contestant.[16]

The point of this exercise isn't to teach students that one version is correct but to encourage them to explore how these two different forms sound and feel to them. Their answers will reflect their own social-class experiences. They might say that one version sounds normal and the other one sounds too fancy. Or they might say that one version sounds normal and the other one too casual. Or they might say that they both sound fine. These responses will reflect their own language use and also other varieties of English that they've been exposed to.

Then what? You could leave it at this, the idea that there are different ways to say the same words. Or you could talk about how other people might react to which version you use. For many elementary and middle school children, this just won't compute; it's just two ways of saying the same thing. But if they recognize that one version is "fancier" than the other, it can lead into a discussion of how people can be judged because of the way they talk and what we can and should do about it.

This is where your own linguistic neutrality is really crucial. If you were to tell students that people are likely to think less of them if they drop *g*'s and therefore they should change their speech, you'd be perpetuating linguistic snobbery. (As well as being disingenuous, since an upper-class person like either President Bush can drop *g*'s with impunity.) However, students' com-

---

[16] You can point out, by the way, that these verbs are normally always spelled with *-ing* even though some speakers read them differently. The exception is when speech is being represented directly and phonetically, as in the possum book.

ing up with their own ideas about people judging others' language is fair game, since they're then free to make their own decisions about their own language and how they look at other people's. This can include:

- I'd never look down on somebody just because they talk different from me.

- What's most important to me is talking the way my friends do, so I can fit in.

- I'm going to start paying more attention to differences in the way people talk, because I think it's interesting.

- As I grow up, I'm going to try to learn how to talk in different ways so I can fit in with different groups.

- I visited another part of the country, or saw the Harry Potter movies where the people were from England, and I wondered why they talked the way they did.

Let's use this same exploratory attitude to think about other social-class features of speech.

Alternative Past-Tense Forms

The examples I'd like to use here are two that are often associated with rural, white working-class speech, *come* and *seen* for simple past tense (*He come over yesterday; I seen him last night*). Both are irregular verbs that change the root word to form the standard past tense rather than adding *-ed*. (*Came* and *saw* are, of course, the more common forms.) Since I've heard them all over North America, I figured they couldn't have occurred by chance in so many separate communities. I posted a question to "Ask a Linguist," which is a service of The Linguist List, an online community. Here's part of Anthea Gupta's answer (2008; full answers from four respondents to my question appear at http://linguistlist.org/ask-ling/message-details1.cfm ?AsklingID=200423242):

Some non-standard forms are older forms of English that are no longer used in Standard English. In other cases, Standard English uses an older form, and a non-standard dialect has an older form. In many cases, the two forms have existed side by side for centuries. This is illustrated by the examples you give. The verbs COME and SEE are both high-frequency verbs with a complex history and many different forms.

The two forms of the past tense ('come' and 'came') are both direct descendants of alternative forms of the past tense that go back to the ancestors of English before English-speakers even came to Britain—we are looking at a competition that is at least 3000 years old! The Oxford English Dictionary has a long discussion on this. But 'came' won in Standard English and is virtually the only form that appears in Standard English texts from about 1500 (the rough time by which there was a single national standard in England).

The past tense of SEE is different—'saw' is the direct descendant of the Old English past tense. But some dialects—from the 1400s—have made the verb more regular by making the past tense and the past participle have the same form, giving rise to a past tense 'seen,' while others have made it more regular by making it 'seed.'

There are now fewer than 200 irregular verbs commonly used in English (Garner, 2009), and some of these forms are likely to change or vanish over the years, particularly less common ones. (It's no surprise today to hear a speaker say *kneeled down* rather than *knelt*.) We're also used to hearing children regularize or change irregular past-tense verbs (*teached, sleeped, brang*). But past-tense *come* and *seen* definitely carry a stigma for middle-class listeners, precisely because they're associated with the people who use them. The reason that those people use them isn't out of ignorance but because of being members of communities that have passed them down for centuries, as Gupta's comments explain in such detail.

If you have students who use these forms, here's a way to approach it. (You can adapt this activity for any other local language features that you've noticed.)

Create two short passages like these and read them aloud:

JOSIE: My friend Sally came over last night. I saw that she was wearing some new shoes, so I asked her where she got them.

SALLY: I was at Josie's house, and then Mary come over. I seen she had new shoes too, so we talked about our shoes.

Ask the students if they notice any difference in the way the two characters talked. If they don't notice, you can point out the alternative verb forms. The most important aspect of the lesson is to build on their preexisting sense of these verbs, which will grow out of their own backgrounds and their speech community's usage. They may well say that the two speakers just said the same thing in two different ways, or they may be aware that they use one form themselves while other people are likely to use the other. Invite them to speculate on why there are two ways of saying the same word. After exploring students' hypotheses, which are likely to focus on the general idiosyncrasy of language, you can then introduce a brief history lesson about how some of the settlers who came to America from England used one form rather than the other, and that this has persisted in the communities where they lived. In my view, this is far enough to take the lesson at this age. It's a chance to appreciate the diversity of language, but mention perhaps that many people consider Josie's usage more "proper." (The next chapter explores language prejudice in more detail.)

Ain't

Let's turn now to a single word. Garner (2009) makes a convincing case that *ain't* still carries a strong stigma unless it's used in specific phrases (*If it ain't broke, don't fix it; It ain't me, babe*), or tongue-in-cheek. He considers usage of it "with a straight face" to be unacceptable English usage. It also, of course, turns up throughout popular culture, not only in representing non-middle-class characters but as one badge of rougher, tougher, or merely more down-to-earth language, particularly in music like rock and hip-hop. The stigma comes primarily, I believe, when *ain't* is used in everyday speech by people for whom it's the default form, who aren't choosing it intentionally. The obviously poor person telling an acquaintance "I ain't had any luck finding an apartment" is in a different class from the *New York Times* blog headline about the 2008 election, "It Ain't Over" (Harshaw, 2008), though note that the word is hardly taboo at the *Times*, or among highly educated people: Ralph L. McNutt Jr., the Mercury Messenger mission's project scientist, was quoted as saying "Mercury ain't the Moon"[17] (June 16, 2011).

> The stigma comes primarily, I believe, when *ain't* is used in everyday speech by people for whom it's the default form.

Historically, *ain't* is a contraction of a number of different forms of *to be* with *not*. It's the only available contracted form of *am not*. (Since we can't say *amn't* and *ain't* is stigmatized, we have to say *I'm not*). In a five-page essay on the word in a usage dictionary (Merriam-Webster, 1989), I discovered that a Reverend John Witherspoon, writing in 1781 in Philadelphia, condemned a whole bunch of contractions that sprang up around the same time: "I will mention the vulgar abbreviations in general, as an't, can't, han't, don't, should'nt, wouldn'nt, could'nt, &c." (p. 61).

I think this opinion would be fun to share with students, since it shows that not only has usage of these contractions changed, but their spelling in some cases has as well. *Han't* is apparently a spelling of *hadn't*, and &c. is, of course, *etc*.

So how should we talk to students about *ain't*, particularly if they use it themselves? First of all, they're almost certain to already know how it's perceived. When I talked to children about it, they were able to clearly articulate that people tend to look down on it and that it's a word people often use in less formal contexts. Both parts of this understanding are important. If you know that a word is considered "bad" in some way, why would you use it? Well, for a lot of reasons: to talk less formally, to sound like the people around you and thus fit in with group norms, and for the fun of self-expression. Similar arguments can be made for cursing; not everybody chooses to use four-letter

---

[17] Note that it's the *New York Times*' choice to capitalize *Moon*; stylistic choices in writing mechanics vary by publication.

words, but those who do have their reasons. If speakers have less experience with formal contexts, they may use *ain't*, curse words, or both in all situations, so they may seem to have a weaker sense of propriety. Our goal here, however, is to help students become conscious of usage features of language, not stigmatize their friends and relatives who use them. So let's move on to the second part of the equation, why *ain't* is viewed negatively in the first place.

As we've seen, there's nothing inherently wrong about the word. Simply put, it's viewed negatively because of who uses it, being historically and traditionally associated with working-class, poor, and African American people. Critics often mention that it sounds uneducated, and those who use it often learn because of school to avoid it, but middle-class kids don't have much *ain't* to unlearn.

I had a discussion about the word with fifth-graders, focusing on its origin, history, and social positioning. Of particular interest to these children, many of whom were Black (African American and from elsewhere), was the connection of *ain't* to the history of slavery. Many features of African American Vernacular English (AAVE, or Black English) reflect that slaves would have picked up English from those British settlers in America who were from the lower social classes. The word then continued to be part of AAVE. (I've written about this same phenomenon earlier in relation to the pronunciation /aks/ for *ask*: Wilde, 1997.) Although the topic can be somewhat uncomfortable, I also talked with the children about how the way that poor people talk is often looked down on compared to the way rich people talk (using simple terminology for social class here, given the age of the students), not because of the language itself but because of who uses it. This was no surprise to these children, who were more from the poor end of the spectrum. Children from richer families also need to learn about this if they don't know it already.

A student's response a week later was revealing. When I came into his classroom, he approached me and told me how his mother had reprimanded him for saying "I ain't going." He informed her, "It's part of my African American heritage" —to which she responded, "I don't care. I still don't want you using it around me." I think this perfectly encapsulates the idea that you may realize that *ain't* can be stigmatized in some contexts, and adjust your usage of it accordingly, but still realize that it doesn't exist in a vacuum, and some people say it because of history.

Double Negatives

Okay, which is easier to understand?

(a) I don't never have no money left by the time I get to the weekend.

(b) I was not unimpressed by his stories.

I find the first one appreciably easier and wonder if you do too, because each negative word strengthens the force of the negativity. It's not true in a sentence like this that two negatives make a positive. (Otherwise we'd have to add up the number of negatives and see if it's odd or even.) Increasing the number of negative words increases the intensity of the negation. In the second sentence, the two negatives do indeed make a positive, but then the listener wonders why the speaker didn't just say "I was impressed." (It's because the double negative is a subtler way to say it, along the lines of "I was impressed even though I hadn't expected to be.")

What am I saying here? That double negatives should be fine in all contexts? Well, maybe they should be, but it doesn't work that way out in the world. My point here is that it's not an issue of logic and clarity but again an issue of social-class prejudice, and any discussion of the linguistic feature should recognize that speakers don't need to have their home language discounted as incorrect. They can just add another variant to it. A good example of this is in *Do You Speak American?* (MacNeil & Cran, 2005), which describes an elementary school classroom with a *Jeopardy!*® game involving code-switching between AAVE and Standard English.[18] (You could also use the terms *informal* and *formal language*.) This book is a companion to a PBS

---

[18] I'd like to define here the way I'm using the term *Standard English*. It's shorthand for society's most widely accepted form of the language, the one often looked for by employers and heard in contexts such as news broadcasts. It's especially associated with, though by no means limited to, middle-class white people with no second-language accent. It's also sometimes referred to as "the language of wider communication" (Delpit, 1995). It's important to realize that "standard" in this context doesn't mean "more correct" but merely the language of the group with higher status in society.

> A good approach to dealing with double negatives and other social-class variations in language among your students is to compile a list of those you hear in their speech.

series that includes a video clip of the classroom exercise (Cran, 2005). The book *Code-Switching* (Wheeler & Swords, 2008) is also a useful resource, as is *Catching Up on Conventions* (Francois & Zonana, 2009).

A good approach to dealing with double negatives and other social-class variations in language among your students is to compile a list of those you hear in their speech and work with them to understand first, the idea of formal and informal language, and second, the more formal equivalents of the way they speak naturally. Given the widespread presence of more middle-class language forms in today's media, most children should be able to recognize if not provide these forms. (It may be a little harder for second-language learners; if they're acquiring the English used in a poor or working-class community, it's an extra burden to take on the nuances of a second dialect, so give them time.) Here are some ideas about how to approach double negatives.

What we want students to learn is that there are two ways that double negatives work in English: they can make a positive or they can make a statement more negative. Philip Larkin's well-known poem "Talking in Bed" (1960; the full text can be found via Google) refers to the difficulty among intimates of finding "Words at once true and kind,/Or not untrue and not unkind." This is a great example of how a double negative makes not quite a positive but a hedged positive. A true and kind statement to your spouse might be "I'm so happy to be married to you"; a not untrue and not unkind one might be "Sure was hot out today." Double negatives can also be intensifiers, however. Wikipedia notes examples where the double negatives make statements stronger and also give them a working-class or tough edge: for instance, the bandits in John Huston's *The Treasure of the Sierra Madre*: "Badges? We ain't got no badges . . . I don't have to show you any stinkin' badges!,"[19] and Pink Floyd's "Another Brick in the Wall," in which schoolchildren chant "We don't need no education/We don't need no thought control."[20]

---

[19] Nicely combining a double negative, a dropped *g*, *ain't*, and ethnic stereotyping. See the YouTube clip.

[20] Also on YouTube.

Begin by posing the question: What's the difference between saying "I was happy" and "I wasn't unhappy"? For instance, if someone asked you what kindergarten had been like, would each of these answers be a little different from each other in what they meant? If the question doesn't make any sense to kids, they don't have enough experience with language to be aware of these forms yet, as they're a fairly subtle feature of English. However, they may be able to put into words something like, "The second one means I didn't hate kindergarten, but it wasn't great either." This is a very small discussion point on a very small feature of English, which may not even be worth talking about at all unless you come across it in literature.

Then show kids the following sentences, and read them aloud with expression, or ask them to.

1. I don't have any money.

2. I don't have no money.

3. I don't ever have any money.

4. I ain't never had no money.

5. I'm broke.

What's the difference between them? Are they just different ways of saying the same thing? Would you understand all of them if someone said them to you? Which one would you be most likely to say if someone asked you for a dollar, or whether you'd ever been rich? Why do you think that we have so many ways of saying the same thing?

Bring out the idea that in English we can use more than one word that means "no" in a sentence (in the above examples, *no, not* [contracted], and *never*). But to some speakers of English, and in more formal contexts, this doesn't sound right, so that the preceding examples 2 and 4 would be considered incorrect. What do you think that's all about? How do they sound to you? This is something to think about in your writing if you want to sound more formal. And if you come across such patterns on a test, double and triple negatives might be considered wrong. (If you're concerned that this could be an issue for test-taking, Google "double negative test items" for some practice examples to talk through. We'll talk about how to explore the language prejudice issues in the next chapter.)

This lesson would work well if students are writing fiction with dialogue in which the characters are from a social group that uses double negatives. They could then explore how to use them artfully. Otherwise, no follow-up or assessment is needed.

Subject-Verb Agreement

Here are two language items from the Common Core State Standards. Both involve demonstrating "command of the conventions of standard English grammar and usage when writing or speaking." For third grade, "Ensure subject-verb and pronoun-antecedent agreement." For fourth grade: "Order adjectives within sentences according to conventional patterns (e.g., a small red bag rather than a red small bag)." Huh? This latter example is the one that makes me most ask, "What problem was this standard meant to solve?" Not only would a native speaker not say "my polo Gap green seven ratty shirts," we'd be extremely hard-pressed to state a rule for adjective order or even to construct one, and have almost certainly never heard of one. Try arranging the adjectives correctly and see if you fit the rule.[21] If not, it's because the "rule" has some flexibility. (This may not come as naturally to English language learners, of course, but that's not who the standards were primarily written for.) This is a clear example of a standard for which no teaching is required because children already know it; it makes no more sense than to set a standard that students should put their lips together when they make an /m/ sound.

But let's look at subject/verb agreement, which plays out a little differently. One third-grader is likely to say "My sister walks home from school" and another "My sister walk home from school." Only the first child will be judged to have met the standard, and this feature is likely to appear as a test item. Yet both children are speaking grammatically in the language of their

---

[21] Quantity or number; quality or opinion; size; age; shape; color; proper adjective, purpose, or qualifier; this list was found on Wikipedia but is also widely available, with some variation, elsewhere on the Web.

home communities. (The reason for this statement is explored more fully in Chapter 5.) However, the standard refers to "the conventions of *standard* English grammar and usage," so one child's home language is less valued and she has a strike against her from the start. (Note that I'm not saying she's disadvantaged; her language is in no way lesser than the other child's, just not accepted in this context.)

How exactly does subject/verb agreement work in English? It's much simpler than it sounds in most explanations. For Standard English:

Third-person singular present tense: He walks. (verb + -*s*)

All other present tense: I/you/we/they walk. (bare verb, no suffix)[22]

Stated even more simply, in the present tense, the bare form of the verb is used except for a third-person singular subject. In other versions of English, particularly AAVE, the (simpler) rule is:

All present tense: I/you/he/we/they walk. (bare verb, no suffix)

There are some situations where correct subject/verb agreement isn't obvious, such as the following: *The teenagers or their teacher (correct/ corrects) their papers,* but these are copy-editor-level niceties, not what the standards are expecting of third-graders[23] Clearly the goal here is to "correct" the language of some children, particularly since the standard applies to speech as well as writing.

There are two other fine points of this discussion. First, in AAVE, speakers can drop the auxiliary in sentences where all versions of English allow it to be contracted. For instance, "they going" is equivalent to "they're going." Second, there's an invariant *be* in AAVE indicating continued action, so that "he's going to church" means he's going right now, where "he be going to church" means he always goes. These aren't errors but alternative syntactic patterns (http://en.wikipedia.org/wiki/Habitual_be).

---

[22] Here are the Standard English forms for auxiliaries: I am, you are, he is, we are, they are; I was, you were, he was, we were, they were; I have, you have, he has, we have, they have; *had, will, would,* and other auxiliaries don't vary.

[23] Would you get this right on a test? The answer is *corrects*; the verb agrees with the subject that is nearer to it.

Presumably curriculum and tests linked to the Common Core State Standards will focus on items that don't appear in all students' home version of English, since these are the ones that some students get "wrong"; indeed, the only native speakers of English who wouldn't meet this and similar standards are those whose versions of English have these slight variations in subject/verb agreement and the use of auxiliaries. (One could say, in fact, that the only reason such test items would exist is to single out these students.) You can do short lessons on these features; for instance, pulling out some sentences from a children's book with third-person-present singular verbs and contrasting them with how the students would say the same thing, but the teacher needs to be aware of why and how the language of children's communities differs from that appearing in curriculum materials and on tests. Perhaps a constructive approach would be to talk with the students directly about language variation, and help them draw on their growing knowledge of the version of English that's considered more formal to be able to code-switch when they choose to, without disparaging the home language.

As a final thought about these five stigmatized features, I'd like to note that if a community is somewhat socially isolated from Standard English speakers, it will be more challenging for children to acquire its speech forms. Labov & Harris (1986) have discovered that some forms of AAVE were becoming more different from Standard English than they used to be as a result of greater social segregation. The most efficient way to have all American children speaking Standard English would be to fully integrate schools, ethnically and by social class. This would also mean, of course, that all children would be likely to become multidialectical, and that Standard English itself would change.

English Language Learners and Usage

The most important idea to remember about English language learners is the obvious and tautological fact that they're still learning English. If you've ever learned a language other than your first one, you know that in addition to learning to produce the sounds correctly, come up with the words, and put sentences together, you have to remember a bunch of little elements that are hard to remember because they don't work that way in your first language. As an English speaker who learned Spanish in high school and French in college, I had to remember to use the right article depending on whether the noun was masculine or feminine, call people by the right pronoun (neither too formal nor too informal), put the adjectives after the nouns, use (in French) two words to make a verb negative, and lots more. Usage, as we've seen so far in this chapter, is often about variation and changes in fine points of the grammatical system, and second language learners are most likely to trip up on those that are different in some way from their first language. (They are also likely to be acquiring the home dialect of their American native-English-speaker peers with whatever usage that includes; many immigrant children in New York City tend to speak English with AAVE features.)

If possible, research your students' home languages to find out what grammatical features of English are likely to be affected. There are many resources available for this; a particularly useful one has tip sheets for language-transfer issues for speakers of ten languages (www.csulb.edu/~rmclaug/en317/1_plan/esl_tips/transfer.html). Teachers of ESL may choose to work on these directly. However, I'd like to speak here about what these special cases of usage mean for the regular classroom teacher and offer some suggestions.

First, learning a second language is largely a matter of acquisition over time, through using the language; colloquial English with many errors comes first and gets better over time. (Krashen, 1982 and Carey, 2007 are especially useful resources on how this takes place and how to support it.) Correction isn't useful and can be inhibiting. Some targeted teaching can be helpful, but more at later stages when the student's English has developed quite a bit and some "teachable moment" instruction focused on a feature or two can come into play. When a second language is involved, there's no stigma attached to not knowing the correct form (unless you're an American talking to a very snooty French person!), so the teaching can be done with a neutral tone.

> Perhaps the most important usage issues facing teachers of English language learners are related to assessment.

Perhaps the most important usage issues facing teachers of English language learners are related to assessment: being careful not to underestimate their abilities because of the language influence, and also not overlooking special needs by assuming that all learning issues are only English-knowledge limitations. In one of the college courses I teach, my students conduct case studies of English language learners. A number of their recent papers mentioned children who appeared to have been placed in reading material that was too easy for them. My students had conducted miscue analyses on them, and it was common to see two kinds of miscues that were likely to have been related to second-language influence: leaving off suffixes, and mispronouncing words whose meaning they apparently knew. If their teachers had used traditional reading assessments such as Qualitative Reading Inventories or Running Record, where an accuracy score is computed, to place them in leveled books, the students' abilities would have been underestimated because of language-transfer features' being counted as errors. There's also a history of English language learners, especially Latinos, being placed in special education classes after being assessed in English (www.usccr.gov/pubs/MinoritiesinSpecialEducation.pdf). Additionally, students who truly do have special needs may be less likely to receive an adequate education if they're English language learners (Fertig, 2009).

For the regular classroom teacher thinking about usage issues for English language learners, what's most important is to recognize language-transfer issues and realize that accompanying usage "errors" shouldn't be foregrounded when they're just part of the student's continuing to learn the language. The Spanish-speaking student who says "Today was snowing" and the Mandarin speaker who says "I have two brother" are both just using forms comparable to those in their first language. Although an ESL teacher may choose to focus instruction on such patterns, they should be accepted in speech and writing as normal developmental features that will decline as knowledge of English increases. Correction of students' speech is never a good idea, for both emotional and cognitive reasons, and this is especially true for students who are doing the best they can with a new language.

Teachers should also do what they can to ensure that English language learners aren't assessed inappropriately in formal testing situations. If they're required to take tests in English, educators need to realize that their potential and knowledge are likely to be underrated, partly hidden because of the language barrier. It's important to be aware that the Common Core State Standards include a statement on English language learners that includes the following: "Teachers should recognize that it is possible to achieve the standards for reading and literature, writing and research, language development, and speaking and listening without manifesting native-like control of conventions and vocabulary." Teachers and schools have to be vigilant that any implementation of the standards includes this recognition.

Usage and Word Choice: It's <u>Alternative</u>, Not <u>Alternate</u>

One other aspect of usage that is worthwhile to think about is word choice, particularly frequently confused words. Often these are words whose meaning has become less distinct over time, and there are a multitude of reference books, many of them enjoyable, that deal with them. In many cases, adults confuse them, and the topic can become very geeky as sticklers insist on a precision of usage that nobody really follows anymore. Here's a litmus test: What's the difference between *alternate* and *alternative*? If you know, you're a vocabulary nerd; these days *alternative* is dropping out of use except in phrases like "alternative rock" or "alternative school," where it carries a connotation of "edgy." *Alternate* is used widely in print as well as speech to talk about situations where there are choices, such as "alternate 401k plans," but it originally actually meant "occurring back and forth in turn," as in alternate lane merging on a highway. Other frequently confused words are those that we don't need to distinguish in speech but may be unsure about in writing, such as *affect* and *effect*. These are a small part of effective writing, can be found in usage manuals, are routinely corrected if needed by copy editors, fall into place as students read more over the years, and aren't usually worth spending instructional time on just because they might come up on a test. (They're also likely to disappear as test items as the language changes, as *shall* has.)

Generational change means that trying to maintain word distinctions that are falling out of favor may be a losing battle. However, there may be some value in exploring these in a limited way with students, particularly around middle school, as an aspect of language and vocabulary development. The best way to go about this is to find a couple of books on frequently confused words and have them in the classroom for reference, pulling out examples for lessons when you feel it would be fun and useful given your students' interest and vocabulary. (See American Heritage, 2004, and Fogarty, 2011.)

Here's an example. What would you want to write on a clothing label or warning sign to let you know that something could easily burst into flames? See what students' responses are. If the only thing they can think of is "This might catch on fire," their vocabularies may not be ready for this lesson yet. However, if they show some knowledge of any variation of the word *flammable*, try this. Write the three words *flammable*, *inflammable*, and *uninflammable*. Ask the students to hypothesize about what they mean and how they're related to each other. Here's the history of them, which is actually pretty interesting. *Inflammable* means, more or less (or did originally), "burst-into-flame-able," related to *inflame*. But people were interpreting the prefix to mean "not," and therefore thinking the word meant "*not* likely to burst into flame." So people in charge of safety starting using *flammable* instead, to avoid this confusion, with *uninflammable* remaining the word for the opposite meaning. This lesson won't teach kids anything they really need in daily life, since usage has now changed so that the words usually used are unambiguous, but it's valuable as an exploration of language for its own sake, which we'll see more of in Chapter 6. Also see Appendix D, at the end of this book, for suggested usage manuals for both kids and adults, with some ideas about how to use them.

A Footnote on Usage: Who's in Charge Here?

Teacher attitudes about language and grammar are part of the picture, too. We all know the stereotype about English teachers, right? We're going to correct people's grammar. (Years ago, at a National Council of Teachers of English convention, Dolly Parton was being honored for her philanthropic work in literacy.[24] She wasn't there in person but had made a video in which she started off by saying, more or less, "I've got to be real careful about my grammar talking to y'all.") But even those teachers who don't see language correctness as a personal crusade are likely to feel a responsibility to help kids learn forms of language that will be acceptable—and make *them* acceptable—in the wider world. But such efforts, if they focus on correction rather than growth and exploration, are likely to be misguided. I'd like to suggest three principles for thinking about and reacting to children's language.

1. Don't be old-fashioned. My classic example of this is the student asking, "Can I go to the bathroom?" and the teacher responding, "Don't you mean 'May I'?" But does anyone really ask permission that way anymore? (Do you ask a friend, "May I borrow a dollar for the Coke machine?") This is the kind of exchange that gives teachers a bad rep!

2. Know what you're talking about. Years ago, the son of a friend of mine had written about "Ulysses's journey" in a school paper. The teacher excoriated him at length for including an *s* after the apostrophe. Well, guess what? The young man's usage was the preferred one for proper names ending in *s* in the usage book I checked (although this rule may be in transition). Sometimes those who are most vigilant about correcting other people's language aren't even right. This also applies to pronouncements like "*Ain't* isn't a word" and "Southerners are lazy talkers."

3. Don't be a language cop in the first place. Correcting kids' oral language (which would, of course, be rude to do with an adult) is often considered appropriate, especially for teachers, on the grounds that this is how learning happens and language improves. But it just isn't true. We talk like

---

[24] Who knew? See www.dollysimaginationlibrary.com/howworks.php for more information.

the people around us talk, and when the way we talk changes, it's because of greater maturity (in the case of young children's speech errors) and exposure to new forms, often coupled with the desire to be part of a new community. Meanwhile, correcting children's language sends a message, even though unintentional, that we're more interested in the form of what they say than the content; this can be very inhibiting and even insulting. It's much healthier to realize that people talk the way they talk, and that polite social interaction recognizes this. We still want to talk about more and less formal language, and to encourage language growth and development, but speech correction is just rude.

I'd like to end this chapter with a story about *can* and *may*, with which Bryan Garner begins the introduction to his handbook, *Garner's Modern American Usage* (2009). After being told by a rental car clerk that an upgrade to a Cadillac might be available, and waiting for her to find out, he asked her, "Can I get the upgrade?" She—astonishingly—corrected him, saying "You mean 'May I get the upgrade?'" (He found the experience surreal, and I imagine his being tempted to say, "Do you know to whom you are speaking?") Of course he meant "Can I?"; that is, "Is the upgrade available?"; he wasn't asking for permission. It's a great example how some of the old, musty rules can end up losing all logic and just becoming a matter of one form's sounding more polite than another. In this case, of course, ironically, the rental car agent was being not only inaccurate but rude.

Language Diversity and Social Justice

In 1990, Peggy McIntosh wrote a now widely known article called "White Privilege: Unpacking the Invisible Knapsack," in which she created a list of 46 assumptions that she could make about her life because she was white, assumptions that people of color were less likely to be able to make. I've rewritten some of these from the point of view of language variation, assumptions that speakers of Standard American English (SAE) can make about their lives. As you read through, think about them from your own perspective. If you speak another version of American English, think about whether you lack these privileges. If you're able to code-switch in and out of SAE, think about whether this has an impact on how you're treated. And if you speak primarily in SAE, think about whether this list rings true.

1. If I call to ask about an apartment for rent, I can be pretty sure that they won't tell me it's no longer available after they hear my voice on the phone. (See Baugh, 2003.)

2. I can turn on the television or radio and hear people who talk like me widely represented.[1]

---

[1] This is changing, in part because there are now so many television channels that advertisers can focus on niche markets.

3. I can be sure that my children will be given literature in school that reflects people that talk like them.

4. I can arrange to protect my children most of the time from people who might not like the way they speak.

5. I can speak in public without being discounted because of the way I speak.

6. I can feel superior to the way other Americans speak.

7. I can be pretty sure that if I ask to talk to "the person in charge," I will be facing a person who talks like me.

8. I can easily buy greeting cards that use the slang or sentimental language of people like me.[2]

9. I can find a job in my field without fear that my language is working against me in the hiring process.

I hope you found this thought experiment useful and sobering. There is indeed language prejudice in American society, and it doesn't exist in a vacuum; it's no accident that the same people who face language prejudice also face other prejudices. Think, for instance, about the different experiences faced in the wider society by someone whose language includes an accent and some words that reflect a Latino background, as compared to an English speaker originally from France.[3]

When I talk about language prejudice with teachers, their immediate response is usually along the lines of "they'll have to be able to use Standard English in a job interview," which, of course, speaks directly to the issue of language privilege. Language variation is a social justice issue just as much as racial identity is. I'll end this chapter by returning to the job interview issue but will first provide the context in which to think about it. The role of

---

[2] This is also changing; the following is from Hallmark's corporate website: "Some cards are bilingual, using a mixture of Spanish and English. They reflect the way many Hispanics speak, especially those ages 18 to 40 that have grown up learning and using both languages."

[3] I'm speaking of the United States here, but it varies by country. For instance, a French-accented speaker will face language prejudice in some communities in Canada.

language in interview situations is in one way the heart of the matter, but in another only the tip of the iceberg.

Myths About Language Variation

There are many attitudes about language in society at large as well as the educational system, and they're for the most part unquestioned and very entrenched. It's human nature to think that the way we and our community speak is normal and that everyone else doesn't sound quite right; they're the ones that have an accent, not us. Whether it's Canadians saying *aboot*,[4] the British talking about the *high street* rather than the *main street*, or the Bostonian calling something a *tonic* that others would just call a *Coke*, it just seems odd to someone from outside the group. But teachers, who often work with students from language communities other than their own, and who are preparing students to live in an increasingly diverse world, need to move beyond this ethnocentrism and take a more sophisticated perspective. Mythbusting is the best way to start.

Myth #1: Standard English Is the Correct Version

Mathematics has right and wrong, but language doesn't, at least not in the sense that this myth promotes. Think of these sentences in terms of correctness:

- You're not the boss of me.
- Please leave me alone.
- Can't nobody push me around.
- Hush and leave me be, y'all.
- Me bothering stop.

Only the last one is incorrect; the first one is slangy, the second one everyday formal, the third one a construction from AAVE and the fourth one Southern

---

4 ⊢ Not exactly what they're saying, but it's perceived that way by most Americans.

English. The last one just isn't an English sentence because the word order is wrong. The rest merely represent different versions of American English. The slang version is acceptable in speech because anyone might say it, but the southern and AAVE ones might be somewhat stigmatized. Why is this? It's an accident of history, and goes back to social-class divisions in Britain, back before the United States existed. When groups of people speaking the same language live in different places or, crucially, constitute subcultures in the same location, their speech diverges. The changes due to location take place for obvious reasons; the United States and Canada were settled by (among others) similar groups from England, but in the few centuries since, American and Canadian English have diverged, although the latter is now, because of proximity, closer to American than to British English.

The social-group changes are more complex. If two groups speaking the same language live in the same city but work in different kinds of employment, live in different neighborhoods, don't mix in school, travel in separate social circles, and each have a sense of solidarity within their group, their versions of English will differ subtly from each other. The more fixed those group differences are in the society, the more their language will become a marker of their identity. The very strong social-class system in Britain is reflected in very distinct language differences, from Cockney to posh. American listeners aren't likely to be too attuned to these differences, but the British know them well. (Britain also has strong regional differences in speech.)

I recently saw a revival of the play *Top Girls* (Churchill, 1984) in London. Afterwards I spoke with two British audience members about how the speech differences between characters, or even one character in two different contexts, signified differences in region and class. These differences (noticeable but not precisely distinguishable to this American's ears) aren't mentioned in the text or stage directions of the play, but were chosen and developed in the production.

The exact same patterns of difference and change have occurred in American speech, even if somewhat less distinctly defined. American speech considered to be different from the "standard" manifests itself by region (most evident in the South, New England, Appalachia, and parts of the New

York City area), by origin (particularly African American but also Native American to some extent), by second-language influence (most prominently Spanish), and by social class. Every individual's language (known as an idiolect) is the sum total of these factors, all of which have to do with the community in which one grew up, particularly peers. Every individual's language also has its own quirks and specificities and reflects her generation as well. To some extent, the groups that sound most like national network news anchors (who are expected to standardize their speech) are considered to speak acceptably, to be the real deal (as it were), with everyone else not quite at that level. To use a linguistic term, news-anchor speech is considered *unmarked*; that is, generic, unaccented, normal, and unremarkable. If you deviate from it, your speech is considered *marked*; that is, it seems to stand out in some way, especially outside your home community.

But who really owns American English? We all do, right? It's not my English, or yours, or Chris Rock's, or Diane Sawyer's, or Sarah Palin's, or the one-year-old's down the street, at least not any of us individually, but all 300+ million of us.[5] (The English language as a whole is owned by many, many more of us all around the world.) So what could be a possible justification for saying that some of these speakers use the language correctly and others don't? Here's where the accident of history comes in. The version of American English that's usually considered correct is one that happens to be used by the social group with the most power. This obviously isn't clearly defined; there isn't a big book in the library that lists the unchanging right way to say everything. But basically the social groups that have the highest income and status are considered to speak correctly while others aren't. (Note that this is about groups; there are plenty of newly rich individuals whose language doesn't conform—think of Snooki—but their children's might well do so someday.) It's not surprising that the "standard" forms of

> But who really owns American English? We all do, right? It's not my English, or yours, or Chris Rock's, or Diane Sawyer's, or Sarah Palin's, or the one-year-old's down the street.

---

[5] Check www.census.gov/main/www/popclock.html for an up-to-the-minute count. It grows by five people every minute or so.

language are also known as the prestige forms. It's not about correctness but about markers that signal where you fit in society.

Myth #2: Standard English Is More Logical

Let's start with an example of Standard English that's been changing over the last few decades. Grammar handbooks would traditionally say that the form "Everyone brought his lunch from home today" was correct and "Everyone brought their lunch today" was wrong. What's the logic to that? *Everyone* clearly refers to more than one person. What changed this usage was the feminist movement to make language more inclusive, which in this case led to more logical wordings. Purists would still say that the "their lunch" wording is wrong, but writers have learned to reword sentences like this to variants like "All the kids brought their lunches," which is not only inclusive but more logical.[6] The traditional rule existed because of convention, not logic.[7]

Double negatives are often called illogical, because supposedly two negatives make a positive. Well, no. Maybe in math (and then only when you're multiplying), not necessarily in language. French uses *ne* before the verb and *pas* after it to negate a sentence. *Never* is expressed by *ne* before the verb and *jamais* (ever) after it, and so on.[8] Nuttier still, there's a different word for *yes* in French if you're answering a negative question. If you were having a good day and were asked "Are you happy?," you'd reply "*oui*," but if asked "You're not happy?," you'd reply "*si*," meaning "Yes, I am indeed." So is Standard English better than French? Well, no, just different. The same when an English speaker says "I ain't never happy." It's not illogical, since no listener would interpret it as meaning that the speaker is always or even sometimes happy; if anything, it makes a stronger statement than "ain't ever" would.

---

[6] There was a period of writing "Everyone brought his or her lunch," and even attempts to invent new pronouns like "Everybody brought tey lunch," but the latter never even had a chance of catching on, and writers, especially copy editors, have figured out that the *he/she* and *s/he* forms are awkward, and that rewording works best.

[7] A purist might say that *everyone* is plural in meaning but singular grammatically, but to the rest of us the old usage just doesn't sound right.

[8] Language is always changing; it's becoming common in informal French to drop the *ne*.

Myth #3: It's About Communication

A common argument made for learning Standard English is that it would make speakers of other versions better able to communicate with others. But it's not about communication. We all speak English, and we all adapt very easily when hearing cadences other than our own. We can watch British movies without subtitles, just as the British can watch American movies. People from all over America, from all groups and social classes, appear on television, which has made mutual understanding of each other's language even greater. (By contrast, in the 1990s, I saw an Irish play in London, which I was enjoying very much, including the accents. I was surprised to hear a British woman tell her friend during the interval [as they call intermission over there] that she could hardly understand anything the actors said. Ireland was closer to her geographically than it was for me, but perhaps its version of English was more distant from her socially than it was for me.)

It is telling that these arguments in favor of a need for communication never think of it as a two-way street; for instance, that physicians from the middle class need to learn other varieties of English so that they can communicate better with a variety of patients. Clearly it's not about communication but about attitudes; it's not that speakers of stigmatized versions of English won't be understood, it's that they'll be judged. There's also something deeply unfair about putting the burden of communication on these speakers, who may also be facing prejudice because of their race or class, since it's far, far easier for the listener to adapt than the speaker. English language learners are criticized for retaining an accent into adulthood, even if they're perfectly comprehensible. Deeply rooted language features that are largely below our conscious awareness, such as accent and some grammatical features, are extremely difficult to change (as any English speakers who have tried to learn a second language know), yet retaining them can be considered as a personal flaw, even though there's no communication problem.

Myth #4: The Earlier You Start Acquiring Standard English the Better

When teachers say kids will need Standard English for job interviews, I agree somewhat (though with the proviso that this may be less true than it used to be; those who do the interviewing have changed over the years). But I hear this not just from high school teachers but from kindergarten teachers! There's a perception that allowing uncorrected "mistakes" in children's speech will just perpetuate them. But language development doesn't work that way.

Here's what I think makes sense in terms of developmentally appropriate practice for helping children add Standard English forms to their repertoire:

- Up through second grade, just let it be. Children in primary grades are still just learning how to read and how to communicate in speech and writing, as mentioned earlier. They're too young to understand why one form of language should be privileged over another.

- The upper elementary grades are a good time to explore concepts like formal and informal language, written language as a more formal register, some simple discussions of language variation (including representing it in dialogue), and the diversity of American English and language in general.

- In middle school, students can work in a more focused way with code-switching and thinking about how to negotiate in a world where their language may be stigmatized.

Middle school and high school are good venues for exploring the social aspects of language variation, as I've talked about in this chapter. As students get older, they can also be encouraged to make their own decisions about what forms of language they want to use in the outside world; we owe it to them to give them all the tools they need to succeed in a world where language prejudice is still rampant, but they may choose not to use those tools.

It's a perfectly legitimate choice to decide not to work for an employer who doesn't accept you as you are, language and all, and we can all hope for a world where all the employers not only accept all versions of English but speak in varied ways themselves. I thought of an analogy to this; a few generations ago, Jewish Americans may have realized, understandably, that changing their names might help them avoid prejudice, particularly in some occupational categories. But it was their choice; Steven Spielberg chose not to change his name, but Ralph Lifshitz (from the Bronx) did. (Google the latter to see what his name is now.)

Now that we've debunked some myths, let's talk about solutions and strategies.

Working with Students With—and Without— Stigmatized Features in Their Language

Back in the day, it was assumed that students needed to change their language to "correct" English. We've fortunately realized that language development is a process of addition, not subtraction and replacement, and that children's home languages are a crucial part of their identity. However, we must continue to interrogate our ideas about where Standard English should fit in to the lives of schoolchildren. I often hear teachers say that home language is okay for the playground but not for the classroom, sometimes reflecting a view that the home language is merely slang. Remember, however, that all versions of American English are equally historically grounded, and that all versions of it include slang but aren't limited to it. Lisa Delpit (in Delpit & Dowdy, 2002) makes the important point that home language is the language of thought, and that to ban it from the classroom[9] inhibits students from fully using language as a thinking tool. Speakers of stigmatized versions of English already face enough prejudice and discrimination in the larger society because of their language; shouldn't the classroom be a haven

---

[9] Which is impossible, of course, because the students speak English; it's just some features of it that teachers want to ban.

of acceptance and respect? This is a different point from preparing them for the outside world's expectations; they can learn to code-switch, but the classroom should be a place where they shouldn't have to.

In addition to the educational issues, we need to remember that in criticizing children's language, you're criticizing their parents' (and community's) language, too, sending a harsh message about who they are and what their value is. This was brought home to me most poignantly when I taught in an Anishinabe (Ojibway) community in Canada in the 1970s. The parents of my students, who were of my generation, had been forced to go to boarding school as children. In addition to the agony of being away from their families all year, they were punished for speaking their own language.[10] As a result, when they grew up and had children of their own, many of them decided to raise them speaking only English so that they wouldn't suffer in the larger world. As a result, fluency in the home language declined dramatically within a single generation. As Nona Ferland (personal communication, 2011), a member of this community, commented recently, "It's really sad that our language had seemed to end with the baby boomers. My parents can't speak Ojibway, but they do understand it. I only understand certain words here and there. I remember my paternal grandparents always speaking to each other in Ojibway but never to us kids. Some people don't realize how much the residential schools and church took from us. We've almost lost our identity, a lot of kids that I teach don't even know that they are Ojibway." Unlike many aboriginal languages, AAVE and other varieties of American English aren't going to die out, but the damage to self-concept that can come from their being disrespected can still persist.

> The societal changes that will make things better for everyone need to involve changes in the attitudes of the groups that are in power.

And for those of you who teach only children who already speak Standard English, and perhaps only Standard English, this section is for you, too. The societal changes that will make things better for everyone

---

10 ▷ The schools were harsh in many ways; Phil Fontaine, who was the elected chief of that community (Sagkeeng) at the time I taught there, became a national Aboriginal leader who helped draw attention to this sad history.

need to involve changes in the attitudes of the groups that are in power. So read on.

Here are some goals for helping students to think about language diversity as a social justice issue. First, we need to name the problem. Second, we need to look at history. Third, we need to see language diversity as a national treasure (in John McWhorter's terms: 1998, p. 154) and celebrate it in ourselves, each other, and our country.

Thinking About Language and Naming the Problem

The premise I'd like to suggest starting with is that it doesn't make sense to say that some Americans talk right and some don't. The video of *Do You Speak American?*, which I mentioned in Chapter 4, is a terrific resource for hearing the range of American speech. It's divided into short segments where the host, Robert McNeil, travels throughout the United States (I enjoyed seeing him use every form of transportation imaginable, from convertible to riverboat) and talks to both ordinary people and scholars about the language he finds there. The program was developed in consultation with linguist Walt Wolfram, well known for his work on American language variation, and its website has resources for educators. I'd also recommend the entire video or the companion book for increasing your own background knowledge about American English. The program's website, with resources, is at www.pbs.org/speak/.

I'd suggest choosing multiple clips that you think would be fun for your students to watch. As you do so, conduct an open-ended discussion about what students think about how their fellow Americans speak—the cadences of their language, the words they use, variations between older people and younger ones.

Then invite them to think about what a space alien who understood English would think hearing all of these different varieties. This could be good as a free-write or turn-and-talk. As you explore these ideas as a group, move students toward the idea that language is one of the many ways that people differ from each other, and that a country's language is the sum total of everyone who speaks it. A second question: What would the space alien say about whose English is best, and what criteria would they use to decide? Give the kids time to explore their ideas: Do they think that one speaker sounds especially cool, or smart, or funny, or on the contrary, odd or unusual? If they think past that one person, and wonder about everyone that lives in the same town as the person on the video, then what? One person may be smarter or funnier than another, but what about everyone else whose language is similar? Also, how does the kids' own language, and that of the people around them, stack up? (Be prepared for a hometown pride reaction like "We talk the best of anyone.")

The point to move toward is that there's no rational way to decide that one version of a language is better than another. We're all used to the way we talk ourselves, which we learned from the people around us, but the people everywhere else are used to the way they talk as well. (And the people who speak other languages all over the world are used to the way they talk too.) A finale for this lesson could be some writing about what the students think of all this. Is it a new idea for them? Do they agree? They may raise questions about why some people really believe that some language is better; invite them to write about that as well, but save the larger discussion of it for the next lesson, after they've had some time to think about it. They might also want to notice the English of the people around them and those they see in the media.

Now that we've looked at language diversity itself, let's talk to students about why some people think that it's a problem. This is a loaded topic, and you'll want to make sure that you handle it with sensitivity, and with a focus on how attitudes about language may unfairly affect how people are treated. The picture book *Don't Say Ain't* (Smalls, 2003) is a possible starting point. It tells the story of a young African American girl who's torn between informal and formal language; a home visit from her teacher, also Black, models code-switching. Although one may not agree with the specific judgment of the book that language like *ain't*

> This is a loaded topic, and you'll want to make sure that you handle it with sensitivity.

shouldn't be used in school, it gives a nice picture of how language can vary for the setting. (One can also choose to talk more formally in different situations even in one's own community; for example, a child on the street in *Yo, Jo!* [Isadora, 2007] is encouraged to talk more formally with his grandfather.)

Don't Say Ain't is specifically about African American characters; the protagonist discovers that the teacher who uses formal language in school is more colloquial on a home visit, even using *ain't* herself. She also realizes that her own language in the neighborhood should fit in with that of her friends, who don't go to her more academic school and have been perceiving her as stuck-up. The book therefore lends itself to exploration of the differences in language used in varying social milieus. After students respond generally to *Don't Say Ain't*, here are some discussion points: Has anyone ever criticized your language? Have you ever felt critical of anyone else's? What's that all about? (The older the students, the more related experience they're likely to have; it will also depend on how much interaction they've had with people unlike themselves.) Make it clear that you're not talking about mistakes in language, like saying *pasghetti* for *spaghetti*, but more just the way you or someone else talks. Next, do you have any knowledge about why people of different social classes may talk differently? You can use examples of different areas in your own community to clarify what you mean. This is uncomfortable material, so think through how your students are likely to react before you raise the question. It might help to think about it as social science, learning about how people interact in a diverse world. Invite them to think about personal experiences and what they know from media. The discussion will obviously vary a great deal depending on the social and economic backgrounds of your students.

Then, a question with no right answer but lots to think about: Do you think people become rich or poor because of they way they talk, or talk the way they do because they're rich or poor? (Economic levels are obviously more varied than this dichotomy would suggest, but this can serve as a framing question.) Here's my answer: social class is somewhat fixed, somewhat mobile. People grow up speaking like those around them, which includes social class. But then their language serves as a marker of their background, and may serve as a barrier when they encounter the gatekeepers to upward mobility, even if there's no conscious prejudice involved.[11]

Well, this isn't fair, is it? But, although not a hard and fast rule in all situations, there's a reality to it. The ideas in this lesson are perhaps the most uncomfortable in this book, but I think they're crucial ideas for teachers to really "get" and pass on to their students. So what are we, as kids, going to do about it? Learn more, come up with our own ways to think about it, and plan ahead for our own lives, whether as gatekeepers, those at the gate, or both.

Some Language History

A passage that I've found interesting to share with children is this one from the book of Matthew, Chapter 7, in the Coverdale Bible, published in 1535:[12] "7 Axe, and it shalbe geuen you: Seke, and ye shall fynde: knocke, and it shalbe opened vnto you. 8 For whosoeuer axeth, receaueth: and he that seketh, fyndeth: and to hym yt knocketh, it shal[be] opened."

I used it with elementary school students, who enjoyed trying to understand it, which involved seeing that spelling (most obviously), grammatical features (the ending -*eth*; the use of *ye* as well as *you*[13]), and sentence structure generally have changed. I chose this passage in particular because it uses *axe* for *ask*, reflecting a pronunciation that was common at the time but has now become stigmatized, but any passage from several centuries ago that retains original spellings will work. (See Wilde, 1997, for a fuller discussion of *axe/ask*; see http://internetshakespeare.uvic.ca/Annex/DraftTxt/ for links to versions of Shakespeare plays with the original spellings.)

The larger history lesson here for students is that the English language has changed over time; see Chapter 6 for further teaching ideas on this topic.

---

[11] Language prejudice also meshes with regional and racial prejudice, which may come into the discussion based on your students' experiences. The tone throughout needs to be one that all versions of English are equally good, but that people who don't know enough about language may not think so, even if they're not personally prejudiced in other ways.

[12] You can make it clear that you're using a passage from the Bible in a way not related to religion but because it's a text from centuries ago that's been preserved.

[13] How would people know which to use when? Hint: *thee/thou/thy* and *ye/you/your* have now been replaced by *you/your* in all cases.

The specific focus here, however, is how history has produced the language variation that we now have in English. Students might find it fun to produce two different modern translations of the passage, one colloquial and one more formal. (Since the passage doesn't have specifically religious content, I think it's appropriate for use in public school settings.) Perhaps. "Ask, and they'll give it to you. Look, and you'll find it," and "Ask, and it will be given to you. Seek, and you will find it." More colloquially still, and loosely paraphrased, "If you ask for it, you're gonna get it; if you look, you're gonna find it." These examples are meant to suggest the range of styles you can help students work toward; the rest of the passage is a little harder and can produce even more variation.[14]

Kids can then talk about what changes they made from the original and how their "modern" versions differ from each other. Then invite them to think about the following question: How did we get from there to here? Some points to think about: The pronouns for *you* have gotten simpler; verb endings have gotten simpler; the word *shall* isn't used much anymore; some people don't pronounce *ask* as *aks* these days. Also, there's something about the way the sentences were put together in 1535 that just sounds a little old-fashioned. Next question: How do you think people reacted when other people started saying just *you* all the time and weren't using *ye, thee,* and *thou* so much? It was probably kids and teenagers who started making the changes first, and the grownups probably thought that they weren't talking right, but gradually everyone talked that way, and now the old ways just seem strange and old-fashioned.

Next question: What do you think happened with *axe* and *ask*? (I'm going to oversimplify a little here in my explanation.) Some people said it one way, some people said it the other way, and maybe they said it one way in one part of town and the other way in another part. The same thing has

---

[14] For comparison purposes, here are two contemporary Bible versions found on biblegateway.com: the typical one in the New King James Version: "Ask, and it will be given to you; seek, and you will find; knock, and it will be opened to you. For everyone who asks receives, and he who seeks finds, and to him who knocks it will be opened." And the *very* loosely paraphrased one in *The Message* (Peterson, 2002): "Don't bargain with God. Be direct. Ask for what you need."

happened with the way we say a lot of other words. Some people who were in England moved to America, starting in 1620. Now all of us in America pronounce some words differently than people in England. What do you think the people in one part of town thought about the way the people talked in the other part? What did the people in England think about the way we changed the language? Maybe the same way that the grownups thought about the kids who weren't saying *ye* anymore back in the day, but what does it matter? Language changes, and one group or generation doesn't have more right to it than anyone else. Language isn't frozen in one time or place. More specifically, *axe* and *ask* ended up diverging by social class. In America, *axe* has persisted most strongly in the descendants of slaves, with a historical link to its use in Britain centuries earlier. And this is probably a good stopping point for this history lesson, although the discussion can certainly continue with your students.

So Now What?

I believe that the best contribution that we can make to create more social justice around language issues is to help create future adults who will appreciate and celebrate the diversity of our language, among both native speakers of English and second language learners, including the immigrants who have always been part of our history. I'll talk first about teaching ideas for those students whose language has been stigmatized, then ideas for everyone, regardless of background.

Students who speak a version of English that some Americans look down on need to realize that the fault is in the others, not themselves, but that even people with good intentions, who aren't prejudiced for the most part, may not understand how language variation works. Social attitudes are changing tremendously, but students may still run across people who feel that their language is "slang," uneducated, rude or improper, "broken," or just plain incorrect. They need to deeply get it themselves that none of these assumptions are justified. It's not even really true that their language is "different," which would assume that there's a norm that they vary from. We *all* speak our own language, it all sounds right in our own communities, and we all own the language, in the sense that all varieties have equal claim to legitimacy. These are linguistic facts.

In the case of English language learners, they're part of a long history of immigration (or, for Native Americans, occupation); if we aren't English language learners ourselves, our parents, grandparents, or earlier forebears were, except for the small percentage of Americans whose ancestors originated only in Britain. It's no more accurate to say that there's one version of English that's the most authentic or important or correct than it would be to say that there's one nationality in the world that's the real deal and to which all others are inferior. England was the first home of English but doesn't own it, just like Africa was the first home of all language but doesn't own it.[15]

The values that go along with these facts should, in my opinion, include recognition of language equality and celebration of the varied ways we express ourselves. For students whose language is stigmatized, that means appreciating their own language and having the knowledge and habits of mind to recognize that criticism of it is unfounded. These students also need (a theme of this book generally) the tools for using forms of English that will allow them to be welcomed in social settings other than their original one, but always with the knowledge that it's not about changing their home language, not about correctness, not even about etiquette, but about getting along in a world that may still judge people unfairly. This is a different issue from becoming more literate, building a bigger vocabulary, expressing yourself with more sophistication, and so on, all of which can be done in any version of English. It's about knowing who you are and the value of what you speak.

For everyone else, to some degree it *is* a matter of etiquette (as well as knowledge and values), not criticizing someone else's language any more than you would their nationality, and in both cases because of knowing that one variation is no better than any other. In practical terms, there are two

---

[15] Think about this as well: the basic human template, originating in Africa, was dark-skinned; light-skinned people came later (Jablonski & Chaplin, 2000). Humans today vary in skin color just like our languages vary from the original language, but we're all fully human.

good ways for teachers to promote this. The first is through having the kinds of discussions that I've suggested throughout this book, and encouraging students to talk about being accepting of everyone's language and not judging them because of it. This also means accepting that the people you know may acquire forms of language that you didn't all grow up with but that reflect their movement into other areas and communities, and that you shouldn't judge people in any direction—because you think they sound less educated, or like a rich person, or like a stranger. This can be the way you approach people not only when you're making friends but when you're hiring them for a job.

In addition to these efforts to inform our students and encourage them to think about values, we can expose them to literature that reflects diverse American language. Appendix F includes a brief discussion of how to look for authenticity in language variation in literature.

Linguistics for Kids

What? Linguistics for kids? In a sense, that's what this whole book is, helping kids learn more about language. The previous chapters, however, focused quite a bit on children's own language, in terms of helping them learn about topics that would directly affect their speech, reading, and writing abilities. This chapter makes a case for pure knowledge, learning about language for its own sake, because it's interesting. Linguistics is a topic that's rarely part of the curriculum, probably because we have so much focus on the *how* of language in school that we've avoided the *what* and *why*. We've talked about language with kids for instrumental reasons—that is, as a tool for reading and writing—in traditional grammar, phonics, and spelling curriculum, but I'm suggesting linguistics as a content area just like (and perhaps as part of) social studies. I'd like to make a case that we should find room for it.

Why would you bother to do this if you're not particularly fascinated by language? Because becoming aware of languages, their own and others', makes kids more attentive to language in practice, and in their own reading and writing. Because turning kids on to the ways language shows up across time and space can move language study from drudgery to fascination. Because learning about language deepens kids' understanding of people and cultures. I've shaped this chapter in the form of questions that we can invite students to explore, questions about the nature, history, geography, and social use of language. I'm by no means trying to cover every possible topic, just some that I think are interesting. For each topic, I'll pose a question and then provide some answers that you can use to conduct a discussion with students, and some resources, including those suitable for children. The exploration of each topic could range in length from a single discussion to a small unit of study.

What Is Language?

In a sense, this is the subject of all the topics in this chapter, but you might want to start with an introduction to this question. Invite students to talk about what it means to speak a language, indeed what it is to speak *using* language in the first place. Where would we be without it? What is language? The most obvious answer: it's what we use to talk to each other (which can be in sign rather than speech). It's also what we read and write. They might find it interesting to consider whether we need language to think. In a way we don't; there's thinking going on when we solve a jigsaw puzzle or play a computer game that may not take a verbal form. But much of our thinking is in words, which may be a big part of the reason why we don't have memories from before we learned to talk. Students could be asked to reflect on, or take notes on, all their occasions for using language during the course of the day: relating to friends and family, reading for pleasure and for information, interacting with strangers when we want or need to, expressing feelings, even in our dreams.

There are three big ideas that you can help them think about to frame their understanding of language. First, all humans have language. There's no community in the world without language, and as far as we know it's been around for a long time, probably 50,000 years or so, although written language is newer (Wells, 2010). Second, only humans have language. Other animals have communication systems, from the ways bees indicate food sources to the warning cries of primates, but they're not language, as we'll see in looking at attempts to teach language to gorillas and chimps. Third, nobody teaches children to talk, they just learn it. Children don't remember their own language acquisition, but they can see it in younger siblings and cousins. They may think they see their parents teaching it ("What's that? Say *doggie.*"), but the learning takes place as long as children are surrounded by language and don't have disabilities that hinder language acquisition. Once they have this foundation, a natural next step is to think about the diversity of language, that just because all humans have language doesn't mean we can speak and understand each other's languages.

How Many Languages Are There in the World?

This is a great starter question, because students are likely to have no idea! When I asked a fourth-grade class, guesses ranged from two or three up to a million. Even the teacher thought perhaps seven; most adults can only guess. I'd begin by posing the question, then hearing students' answers, including their reasoning and any information about the languages they're familiar with. A globe or world map would come in handy here; if you like, you could create a graphic that shows the original locations of languages that they know about. Here's a rundown:[1] There are about 7,000 languages in the world. (The database at ethnologue.com says 6,909 known living languages.) The country of Papua New Guinea has 860 of them. The languages with the most native speakers are, in order, Chinese, Spanish, English, Hindi, Arabic, and Bengali. The numbers of speakers for each are estimates, but (Mandarin) Chinese has more than twice as many speakers as any other language. What counts as a separate language, and distinguishes one from another? Basically, a language is defined by having a community of speakers, which is often but not always limited to a single community. There were 5,260 speakers of the Hopi language of the American Southwest in the 2000 census, 40 of them speaking only Hopi, and their numbers are decreasing. English, by

---

[1] This information comes largely from Facts on File (1996) and Wikipedia, but basic information about the languages of the world is widely available on the Internet. The Linguistic Society of America also has a very readable brief article on the topic (www.lsadc.org/info/pdf_files/howmany.pdf).

contrast, is spoken in many countries around the world and has many varieties, some of them, such as AAVE and those from regions of Great Britain, more fully documented than others. Just as there can be many communities and even countries that use the same language, a single country can contain many languages. The U.S. English Foundation, in a report based on the 2010 census, reported that there are speakers of 322 languages in the United States, reflecting a history of both immigrants and indigenous people (www.usefoundation.org).

To explore this topic with children, I suggest the following ideas; choose one or more, in whatever order makes sense to you. First, conduct a survey of family members and create a graphic representation of languages spoken by students' families, past and present. This could be done on a map, showing the place of origin of each language. Students could also do family trees of the languages spoken by each generation of their family, working backwards from themselves. Students adopted from other countries might have two sets. Some classrooms will have speakers of a variety of languages in the room, while in others, languages other than English may not appear later than the great-grandparents' generation. This topic would fit in well when learning about America's history of immigration.

To check out what languages sound like, go to www.sporcle.com/games/1447/languages_audio, which has an audio quiz with short clips (about 15 seconds each) of 30 languages to identify. Fortunately, there's a "give up?" button to press, so that you can see the names of the languages as you listen to each clip.

The Ethnologue website is a good starting point for students to research individual languages. For instance, I searched by country to find out what languages are spoken in Greenland (Greenlandic Inuktitut 47,800 and Danish 7,830), and then looked up Greenlandic Inuktitut to learn more about it. I then used Google and found audio clips of the related Alaskan Inuktitut, as well as many other materials. Student individual or group projects researching a language could be a great avenue for learning about Internet research, particularly because sites about languages are generally straightforward, with accuracy and bias less of an issue than with other kinds of topics. Languages of the world could be a social studies project that integrates history, geography, and linguistics and could go in a variety of different directions.

The book I'd most recommend as a resource is *The Atlas of Languages* (Comrie, Matthews, & Polinsky, 2003). Although it's an adult book, it's largely readable for middle school students and is full of maps, alphabet and word-family charts, sidebars, and illustrations of people and places, much of it accessible for younger students as well. It's one of the best books on language available to have as a classroom reference.

Where Did Language Come From?

Open this topic for discussion by asking students how we'd get by if we didn't have language. It'd be pretty tough, not just in a modern, postindustrial society, but anywhere. Monkeys and cats and snails get by without language, but we'd be flummoxed. Language is clearly a central piece of being human. People born unable to speak will learn sign language if it's available to them, and deaf children in Nicaragua even invented a sign language, so strongly is language part of our human nature. (More on Nicaraguan sign later.) Next, see if kids have any ideas about how language might have started for the first time. Did our ancestors grunt, as in "caveman" cartoons? Animals are able to communicate with each other in a variety of ways; did early humans just want to communicate badly enough that they invented language, as people wanting to get around more easily invented the wheel?

> Language is clearly a central piece of being human. People born unable to speak will learn sign language if it's available to them.

No, actually, language wasn't invented; it evolved. We'll never know the details, of course, because it occurred in prehistory (by definition, since there wasn't yet any language to write about it in, or even oral history to pass it down in), but a good estimate is that language evolved about 50,000 years ago, around the time period when art was created that suggests cognitive capacities comparable to those needed for language. To have speech as we know it requires a vocal tract that other primates don't have that can produce the speech sounds that we use (Lenneberg, 1967), as well as a certain level of thinking ability. But our brains also appear to be hard-wired for language. One of the pieces of evidence for it (a strong one, I believe) is that every human learns to talk (or sign), barring severe disabilities or social deprivation, and no nonhuman animal does.

It also appears likely that human language evolved just once, in Africa before the diaspora (Wells, 2010) that populated the rest of the world with humans. Here's my hunch as to how it might have happened. A gene mutated, perhaps in one person, since mutations happen by chance.[2] The (let's say) woman with this gene—let's call her Nisa—had children, and half of them inherited the gene; we'll presume it was a dominant gene so that all the children who had it were different in some way from those who didn't, even though their father didn't have the gene. As those children played together, they would have had the extra genetic capacity that enabled them to invent a language.[3] As they grew older, they'd perhaps be more appealing to their peers than their siblings and cousins were, so that the gene would have thrived because of sexual selection (I want to sleep with the guy I can talk to) as well as enabling its owners' success in other ways.[4]

As you explore the origins of language with children, perhaps the most important idea to get across is that language isn't just something we learn like riding a bicycle; it's as deeply imbedded in our human nature as walking is. We don't know exactly how or when it came along, but every society has language, everybody learns how to talk, and anybody could be born into any community and grow up speaking whatever language the people around them speak. The first people ever to talk would have all lived together and spoken the same language, but then people moved all over the world and languages got different from each other. Interestingly, many African lan-

---

[2] Clearly, language isn't the result of just one gene. However, perhaps there was one that provided the tipping point, creating language where previously there had been simpler forms of communication.

[3] This idea comes from Bickerton (2008), who theorized that children are likely to have been the first humans to develop a full language, since they have language acquisition capacities that decline after adolescence. (See also McWhorter, 2011.)

[4] A few months after I wrote this section, I discovered an article in which Noam Chomsky (2010) posited much the same idea (though he called the one person Prometheus).

guages have more sounds than languages in other locations do,[5] so perhaps the first language had a lot of sounds but became phonetically simpler as populations spread (Atkinson, 2011), although this idea is controversial.

Discussion and exploration questions for children: Were people really people before they had language? What would life have been like? If there was a time when some people started talking and others didn't, what would life have been like then? What might have happened over the next 100 years? Let's try spending half an hour without language to see what it's like.

What's the Oldest Language? What's the Newest One? What's the Simplest One? The Most Complicated One?

The oldest language doesn't exist anymore, since all languages change over time. As far as we can figure, all of today's languages are descended from the same ancestor, just like all people have a common ancestor. Language began in Africa, but its descendants are all over the world, with equally ancient lineages. We *can* talk about the oldest written languages (Sumerian cuneiform, followed by Egyptian hieroglyphics), which are inventions.

It's also possible to talk about newest languages. Creoles and pidgins, such as Hawaiian pidgin and Jamaican patois, developed usually among adults who spoke no language in common, particularly in colonial situations. They started out as simple utterances with no real grammar but then gradually transformed into full languages, particularly when they were picked up by children with their greater grammatical capacities. Nicaraguan sign is a new language that was extensively documented by linguists as it unfolded spontaneously in an orphanage in the 1980s, developing among older children and then becoming more sophisticated grammatically as it was picked up by younger ones.

One way to help children realize that all languages are necessarily equally old is through asking them to imagine what English was like in the

---

[5] Some Khoisan languages have more than 100 sounds. Hawaiian has 13, and English has about 40.

past, and then look at examples. You can find children's books from 100 years ago at gutenberg.org; their language is different enough from today's to be noticeable. Here's the beginning of *The Secret Garden*, from 1911:

> When Mary Lennox was sent to Misselthwaite Manor to live with her uncle everybody said she was the most disagreeable-looking child ever seen. It was true, too. She had a little thin face and a little thin body, thin light hair and a sour expression. Her hair was yellow, and her face was yellow because she had been born in India and had always been ill in one way or another. Her father had held a position under the English Government and had always been busy and ill himself, and her mother had been a great beauty who cared only to go to parties and amuse herself with gay people.

Readable, yes (though the older use of the word *gay* would need explaining), but different from today's books. For one thing, the average sentence length of this passage is 22 words. It also just feels different. The "history of the English language" entry on Wikipedia has a few examples of the English of earlier eras; better yet, *Evolving English* (Crystal, 2010), based on an exhibit at the British Library, has dozens of documents of written English from all periods, with commentary, and arranged thematically under topics like dialect and World English. Given this history of great changes in English, students can be invited to think about the other languages of the world, most of which have no written record. If they connect the inevitability of language change with the history of human migration, they'll come to realize that all languages can almost certainly be traced back to a first language.

Speakers of English may think it's complex and hard to learn because we've taken in words from so many other languages. Actually, however, English and other languages that are used widely geographically and acquired by many speakers of other languages tend to become simpler over time; if you learn a language as an adult, it's going to be harder to remember all its bells and whistles, as when an English speaker has trouble attaching gender to words in French or Spanish. These languages then come to reflect this greater simplicity when they're spoken widely by these newer speakers. McWhorter (2011) has terrific examples of how complicated words in smaller, more ingrown communities can become; in Navajo, for instance, the verb for "stink," when it takes the grammatical form *chin*, means "to have taken on a stench to an increasing degree such that one is currently distinctly stinksome" (p. 64). This is, of course, contrary to the stereotype, particularly prevalent in early contacts between Europeans and aboriginal peoples, that the latter's languages were "primitive" and simple.

In exploring these topics with children, an important idea is that language is about variety, not Guinness-book categories like oldest and simplest, because of both the nature of language and its social life. All languages allow human beings to frame and express any ideas they want to, using sounds that our vocal tracts can produce (or signs that our hands can make) and relating words and ideas using some kind of grammar, as well as inventing new words for new things and ideas. All languages then develop their own little quirks, with prefixes and suffixes, unique idioms and expressions, words borrowed and then kept from other languages, new ways of saying things to show that you're part of a new generation or an in-group. It's sort of like fashion in some ways: we're all trying to cover our bodies, but we do so in distinct ways that mutate over time and reflect our identities as members of social groups. The chapter book *Frindle* (Clements, 1996) is a terrific story of a child who invents the word *frindle* for pen and then finds it in the dictionary as an adult, belying his teacher's skepticism. The book is a wonderful stimulus for inviting kids to invent words as a classroom community and see if they can get them to catch on.

> All languages then develop their own little quirks, with prefixes and suffixes, unique idioms and expressions, words borrowed and then kept from other languages.

Is Sign Language Really a Language?

Yes! And there are a lot of children's books about it, including books of signs for babies to learn. (The baby-sign books, however, seem to be targeted to overachiever parents and to focus on single signs rather than a full communication system.) For a long time, it was assumed by many people that the signs used by hearing-impaired people were just a series of crude symbolic gestures. But linguistic research (see particularly Klima and Bellugi, 1979) has demonstrated that it's as full a language as any other, creating a grammar out of hand movement, location, word order, facial expression, and other elements.[6] It may be one of the more useful second languages for American students to learn, although it's been slow to gain acceptance for school and college language requirements, perhaps because it doesn't have a written literature.[7] Now that students with special needs, including those with hearing impairments, have been more integrated in schools, kids are especially likely to want to learn about sign.

The book *Sign Language for Kids* (Heller, 2004) is a good introduction to the topic for children. Try beginning with a discussion of sign generally. Who uses it and why? Do some hearing people use it? If so, why? How do you think Deaf[8] and hearing people learn it? Do you think it's really a language? After the discussion, the book can answer these questions as well as teaching the students a lot of signs, not just simple words but sentences and expressions. An outstanding middle-grades novel, *Wonderstruck* (Selznick, 2011) includes Deaf characters and the use of sign language, which the author has researched and informs the reader about.

One fact that's important for both students and teachers to know is that students whose first language is American Sign Language (ASL) learn English as a second language. ASL isn't just signed English, which is a pidgin sign using signed words but English word order, often used by the hearing to communicate with ASL users. Using children's books can help students learn signs but also realize ASL is a full language.

---

[6] Note that there are multiple sign languages. For instance, American Sign Language (ASL) is completely different from British sign but similar to French sign for historical reasons.

[7] See www.gallaudet.edu/library/deaf_research_help/frequently_asked_questions_%28faqs%29/sign_language/asl_academic_acceptance_and_official_recognition.html for information about which states recognize ASL as a language for various purposes.

[8] *Deaf*, when capitalized, is conventionally used to refer to hearing-impaired people in a broad sense of their identity, which involves a culture, not just a physical characteristic.

Where Does the Alphabet Come From, and Why Doesn't Everyone Use the Same One?

There have been a lot of different writing systems throughout history, and many books have been written about them. The earliest that we have records of is Sumerian cuneiform, dating back to around 3400 BC. *The Atlas of Languages* (2003) has a good illustrated chapter on writing systems. Only a relatively small number of languages developed written forms, many of them independently of one another. Many are alphabetic, where every symbol represents a sound (more or less), while others represent syllables or words, with Chinese being the best-known example of the latter, although it's not purely ideographic (word-representing) anymore. A good children's book about the history of the alphabet is *Alphabetical Order* (Samoyault, 1998; see also the companion book, *Give Me a Sign*, 1997). The picture-book biography *Sequoyah* (Rumford, 2004) tells the story of the Cherokee who invented a syllabic writing system for his language.

Rather than just seeing examples of other alphabets, students might benefit from looking at children's books in other writing systems, particularly if they can be compared side-by-side with the English version or are bilingual. (I have a copy of the lift-the-flap classic *Where's Spot?* in Arabic; it goes from back to front.) If your local library doesn't have any, an Amazon search for, for instance, "Arabic English children's books" will turn up multiple bilingual titles, many of them alphabet and word books that will make comparisons easy and be interesting even for older children. Looking at newspapers and other periodicals written in other alphabets (available in most communities with immigrant populations and also online) can also provide an interesting peek into a different linguistic environment.

So why don't we all use the same alphabet? With expanded worldwide communications, it would be helpful, but digital technology is making it less necessary. When I Googled "Hindi newspaper," the first link was to the site www.bhaskar.com, which was in Hindi, but the link also offered the "translate this page" option, which instantaneously took me to the same page in English. It's also possible, of course, to use keyboards to type in any alphabet.

The cultural spread of English has of course made our (Roman) alphabet more prevalent, with English a common second language all over the world, but there's no reason that people who speak Arabic, for instance, should switch to our alphabet any more than we should switch to theirs. Distinct writing systems developed on their own (unlike speech, which has a common origin) for historical and cultural reasons, just like different cuisines, but we aren't likely to have fusion alphabets the way we have fusion restaurants. The Japanese language actually uses three writing systems, reflecting its history, but this is unusual.

Is It True That People Taught Gorillas and Chimpanzees to Use Language?

Well, no. These experiments are generally considered to have failed. I sometimes share with teachers one of two children's books by Francine Patterson, *Koko's Story* (1988) or *Koko's Kitten* (1987), which describe in a kid-friendly way her experiences teaching sign language to a gorilla. I split the teachers into two groups and ask each one to present either the case that what Koko learned was indeed language, or that it wasn't, and to present their best arguments. I point out that the fact that it's not oral doesn't matter, since gorillas' vocal tracts don't allow them to make human speech sounds. The students are able to make the case for either side, but clearly most of them believed that Koko did indeed learn language; they typically say that she's clearly communicating.

Children are likely to enjoy the Koko books, which are cute and charming. But to those who know anything about language, they're a terrible example of anthropomorphizing; that is, attributing human behavior to animals. The consensus of linguists is that, although nonhuman primates were indeed able to learn individual signs, they were never able to put them together into anything remotely resembling human language, in part because they never developed syntax or other complex features, at best stringing several signs together but never into anything like a sentence. Claims of anything else were wishful thinking on the part of their trainers, and Patterson was, and continues to be, especially guilty of this. (Koko is alive and well and living on Maui, and Patterson does important work in species preservation; see koko.org.) Rereading the picture books through a more critical lens, one can see that she makes big leaps beyond what her data show, interpreting some of Koko's signing as lying or making jokes despite the lack of any evidence of intentionality on Koko's part. Was Koko "playing a joke" when she signed "that red" while playing with white towels, then picked a red speck of lint off one of them, or did the researchers just not realize what she was looking at? And as I say to teachers, Koko may sign the word string "love lunch eat taste it meat" when prompted for a long sentence about lunch, but that's a long way from saying, "Gee, boss, I'm glad our grant was renewed so that we can stay on Maui for the rest of my life." (For a good brief discussion of the primate language experiments, see Pinker, 1995.)

I'd definitely share the Koko books and website, which includes videos, with children, because they're very appealing. However, I'd start with a discussion about whether they think animals can be taught language by humans, and what they'd look for as evidence that this had taken place. Then they can watch the videos and read the books intelligently, as an exercise in critical reading and listening.

I'd also recommend, for your own reading, *Nim Chimpsky* (Hess, 2008), as well as the documentary film based on it, *Project Nim* (2011), about attempts in the 1970s to teach sign language to a chimpanzee. They're less about language, however, than about the human and animal-welfare stories involved in the research, including Nim's smoking marijuana with the researchers (captured on film) and physically attacking some of them. The film, with lots of terrific archival footage, never gave me any sense that Nim's signing was language-like in any way. Word recognition, maybe, but that's it; even the chief researcher, Herbert Terrace, decided that it was a failed experiment.

Where Do People's Names Come From?

Human naming practices are a small but important part of language. Surnames have a variety of different origins; one simple type is that a form of a parent's first name becomes his children's last name, as in many Scandinavian countries. In Iceland, typically the son of a guy named Jon will have Jonsson as his last name, while Jon's daughter's surname will be Jonsdottir.[9] Other surnames came from an occupation (Smith) or a dwelling place (Rivers); those from other languages may work the same way, such as the French Lefevre (ironsmith) or the Spanish Guerrero (warrior).

There are lots of books about the origins and meanings of first names, particularly for prospective parents looking for baby names. Babynames .com is riddled with ads, but you can search names generally and find out their origin, as well as looking at names from various languages; there's actually a list of Aztec names, including Tupac. Social Security has a great website for exploring the popularity of names over the years (www.ssa.gov/oact/babynames/). I never asked my parents why they named me Sandra, but a quick search showed me that it was the sixth most popular name the year I was born; its popularity has dropped steadily and it's now 517th. Spanish names are growing in popularity in the United States as the Latino population increases.

> There are histories of naming practices for particular cultures within America.

There are histories of naming practices for particular cultures within America. Jewish families often name children after deceased relatives. In the late 18th and 19th centuries, many European Jews, who had traditionally used patronymic (father-indicating) surnames, were required by authorities to take on European names so that they could be better accounted for by governments (Kaplan & Bernays, 1997). Some countries control what names people are allowed to have; I've met a woman from Japan (living in the United States) named Reiko who tried to change the spelling to Rayco, but when she went to the Japanese consulate to

---

9 ⊢ Sometimes the mother's name is used as a surname, so that the singer Bjork's daughter could have Bjorksdottir as her last name.

try to change it on her passport, they wouldn't let her because the spelling was un-Japanese.

African Americans often give children distinctive names, perhaps with an African origin or Afrocentric sound to them. Sometimes they want to give children unique names, because of the history of names being obliterated during slavery (Kaplan & Bernays, 1997). These African American names have sometimes, unfortunately, been the object of derision; I've heard teachers say that children with names like Taniqua and Deonte may have trouble getting jobs as adults, but more and more people with names like those will be not only in the job market but the ones doing the hiring, so such prejudices will decline. As Americans, we've learned over the centuries to get familiar with new names (Nguyen was the fastest-growing surname in the United States from 1990 to 2000), and we'll continue to do so.

Celebrities have been castigated in the media for giving their children odd names, such as Gwyneth Paltrow's daughter Apple, but naming practices seem to be getting more open-ended all the time. Kids can always change their names when they get older. The film director Duncan Jones (*Source Code*, 2011, b. 1971) is apparently using his actual birth name, but his father David Bowie was notorious for supposedly naming him Zowie Bowie, the name he was known by as a child. Similarly, Yippie Abbie Hoffman's son america (sic) now goes by Alan, but rocker Grace Slick's daughter China Kantner (b. 1971) has kept her name.

The best way to explore this topic with children is to start by asking them what they know about where their names, both first and last, came from, and to talk about what they might like to name their children when they have them. I had a great discussion with some intermediate-grade students about what they knew about how their parents picked their names and what names they might choose for their own children when they grew up. This is also obviously a good topic for kids to talk about at home, and wouldn't it be a terrific topic for a family night at school? Students can also use the phonebook to see what surnames are particularly common where they live, and to check out the origins of names they see in the news.

President Barack Hussein Obama, named after his father, went by Barry as a boy but then reverted to his given name as an adult. Why do people change their names during their lifetime? Malcolm X (born Malcolm Little) is a vivid example of this. President Bill Clinton was born William Jefferson Blythe III; what's his story? Should women change their names when they get married? Whose last names do children bear and why? Why do people in some countries, like Indonesia and Afghanistan, have just a single name? (When President Suharto of Indonesia died in 2008, I stumped people by asking them what his first name was. He didn't have one, nor did Indonesia's first president, Sukarno.)

Will We All Speak the Same Language Someday?

Our lives are getting more global all the time, so that we might wonder if we could all become one big culture with the same language one day. Also, and sadly, many smaller languages are disappearing. It would make things easier to have a single language, wouldn't it? But everything we've discussed in this book suggests that it would be very, very unlikely. First of all, there are more people all the time; the world's population is approaching 7 billion. (The United Nations projects that it will peak at 9.22 billion in 2075, though this seems oddly precise; www.un.org/esa/population/publications/longrange2/WorldPop2300final.pdf.) More people mean more speech communities. A nomadic culture's communities are small enough to know everyone by name, but the United States has many high schools and workplaces, each cohesive enough to develop some of its own lingo. Counterforces to this splintering of language come, of course, from mobility and interconnectedness, so that humans may know many people over the course of a lifetime and connect electronically with many more; time will tell what effects this has on language. Remember also, of course, that there's generational as well as locational change in language. Teenagers in Shenzhen, Nairobi, and Dubuque all want to talk a little differently than their parents do.

It's hard, however, to imagine how we'd get to the point of only one language. English is becoming more of a world language than ever, but it reads and especially sounds different everywhere that it's used, as each speech community makes it its own. But let's imagine a thought experiment, where everyone in the world woke up one morning speaking Chinese, and only Chinese, in the same way, as a native speaker.[10] Let's say that all the written language in the world would change too. Guess what? It wouldn't last. People in West Virginia and in Krakow would come up with their own little ways of saying things. Teenagers in Auckland and Nome would develop new slang. Everybody would watch the same TV shows from all over for a while, but people in Cairo would start complaining about the accents and "bad grammar" of the people filmed in La Paz and vice versa. In a few hundred years or so it would be harder to understand one another and hard to read books written around the time the change first happened. In thousands of years (give or take) we'd be back to thousands of languages again.

Two teaching ideas: First, invite kids to think, talk, and write about this thought experiment. It could be part of a study of science fiction, speculative fiction grounded in scientific accuracy, in this case the nature of human language. Second, learn something about disappearing languages, many of them aboriginal languages of North America. *National Geographic* has a terrific website and project on the topic (http://travel.nationalgeographic.com/travel/enduring-voices/), which includes links to language-preservation programs. Although American immigrant populations may not include speakers of endangered languages, students can research those from states or countries they've visited or that their people came from. There's also a book that grew out of the National Geographic project, *The Last Speakers* (Harrison, 2010). Another useful book for teacher background is *Vanishing Voices* (Nettle, 2000), which talks about how language extinction often goes hand in hand with habitat destruction and other forms of endangerment.

I believe that the topic of language loss is likely to be of strong interest to children because of its parallels to plant and animal loss; languages become

---

10 - I've of course picked Chinese, since it's the world's most common language.

> Languages become endangered just as life forms do, and the extinction of a language is a tragedy as much as extinction of a species because of knowledge lost that can never be regained.

endangered just as life forms do, and the extinction of a language is a tragedy as much as extinction of a species because of knowledge lost that can never be regained. The two books cited previously give numerous examples of this; for instance, the Tofa language of Siberia reflects extensive knowledge of the reindeer that are a staple hunting prey in the culture. Astonishingly, *dönggür,* means "male domesticated rideable reindeer in its third year and first mating season, but not ready for mating." Reviving an extinct language doesn't do the trick when its original native speakers are all gone; a language revived from extinction can't ever be the same language.

Thinking about the many languages of the world and paying some attention to those that are vanishing is perhaps a fitting way to end this book, since I hope I've inspired you with an appreciation of language diversity, in our own country and throughout the world. The teaching of grammar has typically been a conservative enterprise, trying to fit everyone to a single standard. It's also implicitly lent support to conservative views of language out in the world, not only judging people on their language but attributing language differences to lack of knowledge or intellectual prowess. But in reality, language is wild and free, deeply reflecting both our common birthright as humans and all our differences of culture, generation, and individual quirkiness. Language study isn't about being picky grammarians, it's about exploring, appreciating, and enjoying the essential nature of our diverse humanity.

Appendix A:
Language Curriculum Year by Year

Most of the activities described in this book can be adapted for a variety of different grade levels, but I'm providing here a suggested outline of what topics you might wish to cover in grades 3–4, 5–6, and 7–8, perhaps particularly useful if you're trying to coordinate across grade levels. For each grade, I've suggested what you might want to include for each of the four major topics of this book: mechanics, grammar, usage, and linguistics. There's no set amount of time to spend on each one; you might choose to just cover some basics, or do a deeper exploration if you and the students are interested. I've italicized those that are related to Common Core State Standards for that grade level.[1]

Although I've taken developmental appropriateness into account, these are merely suggestions; any topic could be explored appropriately at a variety of grade levels.

---

[1] The following are included in the Common Core State Standards for grades 11–12, and are connected to these topics that I'm suggesting for grades 7–8: Apply the understanding that usage is a matter of convention, can change over time, and is sometimes contested; Resolve issues of complex or contested usage, consulting references (e.g., Merriam-Webster's *Dictionary of English Usage*, *Garner's Modern American Usage*) as needed.

	3–4	5–6	7–8
Mechanics	*Capitals and apostrophes* Sentence punctuation Text features Punctuation for fun	Punctuation in longer sentences; paragraphing Basic bibliographic citation *Punctuation for effect*	Longer sentences Fragments and run-ons Advanced bibliographic citation Complex text features for expository writing
Grammar	*Parts of speech (nouns, pronouns, verbs, adjectives, adverbs)* *Verb tenses (past, present, and future)*	*Parts of speech (conjunctions, prepositions, interjections)* Verb tenses (all 16 tenses) *Sentence expansion and contraction*	Verb tenses (understanding how they're connected) Sentence combining
Usage	Language variety *Code-switching: formal and informal language*	*African American Vernacular English (for all students; in more depth for those who speak it)* *Code-switching: generational and cultural differences* Language change	Language prejudice and social justice Code-switching: making choices about your own language
Linguistics	What is language? How many languages are there in the world? Where do people's names come from?	Is sign language really a language? Is it true that people taught gorillas and chimpanzees to use language? Where does the alphabet come from, and why doesn't everyone use the same one?	What's the oldest language? What's the newest one? What's the simplest one? The most complicated one? Where did language come from? Will we all speak the same language someday?

Appendix B:
The Common Core State Standards

The Common Core State Standards relevant to this book, those in the area of language, are broken down into three categories: conventions of Standard English, knowledge of language, and vocabulary acquisition and use.[2] Since they're focused on what students should be able to do at different grade levels, they aren't equivalent to a curriculum map, let alone a full scope of content in the area of language, or a guide to instructional methodology.

First, they're a mixture of knowledge and abilities that children will acquire (indeed, will have largely already acquired) just through using language, and those that they won't. Examples of each, from the third-grade standards, are "Use abstract nouns (e.g., *childhood*)" and "Explain the function of nouns, pronouns, verbs, adjectives, and adverbs in general and their functions in particular sentences." If kids have talked about friendship and kindness, they've used abstract nouns, but they don't necessarily know that they're nouns. (See Chapter 3 for a discussion of learning about the names of parts of speech.) One problem with operationalizing the standards is that schools are likely to think that all of them need to be *taught*, even if kids have already acquired them. In practice, a third-grade teacher need only (at most) check off whether her students are using abstract nouns and other features mentioned that are part of normal language acquisition, as indicated in the chart below. (This doesn't, however, mean that English language learners, who may not yet have acquired all of these features, should be taught them formally, as I've discussed on pp. 88–90.)

Second, in some cases, the standards were apparently meant to solve a particular problem that's narrower than what the standard as a whole implies. One example, from the sixth-grade standards: "Ensure that pronouns are in the proper case (subjective, objective, possessive)." For the most part, this already happens. Sixth-graders aren't saying "I have mine book" (using the wrong pronoun case) instead of "I have my book," any more than they'd say "Book I my have" (using the wrong word order). However, they do say and perhaps write "Me and Juan played baseball," "Who did you call?," and "It's him." When you look on websites like dailygrammar.com, one of the first results in a Google search for "pronoun case lessons," there are five tedious lessons describing pronoun case in general and providing exercises. Com-

---

2 - The vocabulary standards are beyond the scope of this book, but many of these comments apply to them as well.

pletely pointless; the standards aren't asking for kids to be grammarians on this one, nor should they be. I've discussed the specific examples of pronoun case usage that the standards appear to be targeting on pp. 71–74.

Third, some of the standards are so simple that you can easily develop brief, targeted lessons on them yourself or find ideas on the Internet or in published sources. For instance, I didn't think it was necessary to include a lesson in this book on using commas in addresses since the rules are so simple and rarely used. Indeed, on envelopes, where we're mostly likely to write addresses, the U.S. Postal Service prefers no punctuation. (For email addresses, what's needed isn't rules but the exact, verbatim address.)

Fourth, there are items in the Common Core State Standards that don't seem worth teaching. They seem to have been developed in large part through looking at traditional grammars of English, without much attention to their importance for writing, developmental appropriateness, or even accuracy (for instance, the comma between coordinate adjectives is often omitted in standard usage). Some of these are proofreading details that would be attended to by a copy editor for published writing, but aren't relevant for students at these levels. Others involve grammatical terminology that has no practical application (e.g., explaining participles). These could come up on a test, but I can't recommend teaching them for other reasons.

I therefore present a table in which I've identified each element from the "Language" sections of the Common Core State Standards for grades 3–8 that fall within the scope of this book[3] and tagged them in four categories. Column A of the table indicates those standards that are addressed directly in this book, with page references. In some cases, such as pronoun case, students already have much of the knowledge that the standard covers, so only need some narrowly targeted instruction.

The second column indicates standards that involve aspects of language that children pick up as part of speech acquisition or, for some of the middle-school items, through development of the writing process generally. They don't need to be taught. Column C includes minor items that you can easily address. Column D is for items that I don't believe are worth teaching because they're pointless or inappropriate

---

[3] This includes the sections on Conventions of Standards English (except the spelling sections, which I've explored in other books [Wilde, 1992, 1996, 2008]), and Knowledge of Language.

Third grade

	A — Addressed in this book	B — Part of language acquisition	C — Short, targeted lesson	D — Not worth teaching
1. Demonstrate command of the conventions of standard English grammar and usage when writing or speaking.				
a. Explain the function of nouns, pronouns, verbs, adjectives, and adverbs in general and their functions in particular sentences.	✓ (28–30, 152–154)			
b. Form and use regular and irregular plural nouns.				
c. Use abstract nouns (e.g., childhood).		✓		
d. Form and use regular and irregular verbs.		✓		
e. Form and use the simple (e.g., I walked; I walk; I will walk) verb tenses.		✓		
f. Ensure subject-verb and pronoun-antecedent agreement.	✓ (86–88)			
g. Form and use comparative and superlative adjectives and adverbs and choose between them depending on what is to be modified.	✓ (69–71)			
h. Use coordinating and subordinating conjunctions.		✓		
i. Produce simple, compound, and complex sentences.	✓ (50–54)			
2. Demonstrate command of the conventions of standard English capitalization, punctuation, and spelling when writing.				
a. Capitalize appropriate words in titles.			✓	
b. Use commas in addresses.			✓	
c. Use commas and quotation marks in dialogue.	✓ (28)		✓	
d. Form and use possessives.				
3. Use knowledge of language and its conventions when writing, speaking, reading, or listening.				
a. Choose words and phrases for effect.		✓		
b. Recognize and observe differences between the conventions of spoken and written standard English.	✓ (Ch. 4)			

	A—Addressed in this book	B—Part of language acquisition	C—Short, targeted lesson	D—Not worth teaching
Fourth grade				
1. Demonstrate command of the conventions of standard English grammar and usage when writing or speaking.				
a. Use relative pronouns (who, whose, whom, which, that) and relative adverbs (where, when, why).		✓		
b. Form and use the progressive (e.g., I was walking; I am walking; I will be walking) verb tenses.		✓		
c. Use modal auxiliaries (e.g., can, may, must) to convey various conditions.		✓		
d. Order adjectives within sentences according to conventional patterns (e.g., a small red bag rather than a red small bag).	✓ (86–87)			
e. Form and use prepositional phrases.		✓		
f. Produce complete sentences.	✓ (18–20)			
2. Demonstrate command of the conventions of standard English capitalization and spelling when writing.				
a. Use correct capitalization.			✓	
b. Use commas and quotation marks to mark direct speech and quotations from a text.			✓	
c. Use a comma before a coordinating conjunction in a compound sentence.			✓	
3. Use knowledge of language and its conventions when writing, speaking, reading, or listening.				
a. Choose words and phrases to convey ideas precisely.		✓		
b. Choose punctuation for effect.			✓	
c. Differentiate between contexts that call for formal English (e.g., presenting ideas) and situations where informal discourse is appropriate (e.g., small-group discussion).				

Fifth grade

	A — Addressed in this book	B — Part of language acquisition	C — Short, targeted lesson	D — Not worth teaching
1. Demonstrate command of the conventions of standard English grammar and usage when writing or speaking.				
a. Explain the function of conjunctions, prepositions, and interjections in general and their function in particular sentences.				
b. Form and use the perfect (e.g., I had walked; I have walked; I will have walked) verb tenses.	✓ (36–43)	✓		
c. Use verb tense to convey various times, sequences, states, and conditions.				
d. Recognize and correct inappropriate shifts in verb tense.			✓	
e. Use correlative conjunctions (e.g., either/or, neither/nor).			✓	
2. Demonstrate command of the conventions of standard English capitalization, punctuation, and spelling when writing.				
a. Use punctuation to separate items in a series.				
b. Use a comma to separate an introductory element from the rest of the sentence.				
c. Use a comma to set off the words yes and no (e.g., Yes, thank you) to set off a tag question from the rest of the sentence (e.g., 's true, isn't it?), and to indicate direct address (e.g., Is that you, Steve?).			✓	
d. Use underlining, quotation marks, or italics to indicate titles of works.	✓ (144–145)		✓	
3. Use knowledge of language and its conventions when writing, speaking, reading, or listening.				
a. Expand, combine, and reduce sentences for meaning, reader/listener interest, and style.	✓ (54–57)		✓	
b. Compare and contrast the varieties of English (e.g., dialects, registers) used in stories, dramas, or poems.	✓ (Ch. 4, 160–162)			

	A—Addressed in this book	B—Part of language acquisition	C—Short, targeted lesson	D—Not worth teaching
Sixth grade				
1. Demonstrate command of the conventions of standard English grammar and usage when writing or speaking.				
a. Ensure that pronouns are in the proper case (subjective, objective, possessive).	✓ (71–74)			
b. Use intensive pronouns (e.g., myself, ourselves).		✓		
c. Recognize and correct inappropriate shifts in pronoun number and person.	✓ (100)			
d. Recognize and correct vague pronouns (i.e., ones with unclear or ambiguous antecedents).			✓	
e. Recognize variations from standard English in their own and others' writing and speaking.	✓ (Ch. 4 & 5)		✓	
2. Demonstrate command of the conventions of standard English capitalization, and spelling when writing.				
a. Use punctuation (commas, parentheses, dashes) to set off nonrestrictive/parenthetical elements.			✓	
3. Use knowledge of language and its conventions when writing, reading, speaking, or listening. ()				
a. Vary sentence patterns for meaning,	✓ (54–57)			
b. Maintain consistency in style and tone.		✓		

/ 138 /

	A—Addressed in this book	B—Part of language acquisition	C—Short, targeted lesson	D—Not worth teaching
Seventh grade				
1. Demonstrate command of the conventions of standard English grammar and usage when writing or speaking.				
a. Explain the function of phrases and clauses in general and their function in specific sentences.				
b. Choose among simple, complex, and compound-complex sentences to signal differing relationships among ideas.				
c. Place phrases and clauses within a sentence, recognizing and correcting misplaced and dangling modifiers.	✓			
2. Demonstrate command of the conventions of standard English capitalization, and spelling when writing.				
a. Use a comma to separate coordinate adjectives (e.g., It was a fascinating, enjoyable movie but not He wore an old[,] green shirt).			✓	
3. Use knowledge of language and its conventions when writing, reading, or listening.				✓
a. Choose language that expresses ideas precisely and concisely, recognizing and eliminating wordiness and redundancy.				

Eighth grade

	A—Addressed in this book	B—Part of language acquisition	C—Short, targeted lesson	D—Not worth teaching
1. Demonstrate command of the conventions of standard English grammar and usage when writing or speaking.				
a. Explain the function of verbals (gerunds, participles, infinitives) in general and their function in particular sentences.				✓
b. Form and use verbs in the active and passive voice.		✓		
c. Form and use verbs in the indicative, imperative, interrogative, conditional, and subjunctive mood.		✓		✓
d. Recognize and correct inappropriate shifts in verb voice and mood.				✓
2. Demonstrate command of the conventions of standard English capitalization, punctuation, and spelling when writing.				
a. Use punctuation (comma, ellipsis, dash) to indicate a pause or break.			✓	
b. Use an ellipsis to indicate an omission.			✓	
3. Use knowledge of language and its conventions when writing.				
a. Use verbs in the active and passive voice and in the conditional and subjunctive mood to achieve particular effects (e.g., emphasizing the actor or the action; expressing uncertainty or describing a state contrary to fact).		✓		

Appendix C: Text Features for Student Writing: A Style Guide

As part of learning about conventions of writing, I've provided a simple style guide that students can use for citations and reference lists, particularly in informational writing. It's meant to be simple enough for children in these grades to use, but accurate and reasonably complete. For citations more complicated than books, magazine articles, and websites, I'd recommend the Purdue OWL's American Psychological Association (APA) format website (http://owl.english.purdue.edu/owl/resource/560/1/). I've also included a section on when and how to use quotations that provides a brief introduction to academic integrity.

The Kids' Guide to Citations and Reference Lists

When you read books that are about facts and other kinds of information, where the author got ideas from reading, interviewing people, or other information outside of his or her own head, there are *text features* that show you where the information comes from and how to find it. This guide is a reference for you to use when you're writing about information.

Information from Other People

Citation means that when you get information from another person—whether you talked to them, read their book, or read their website—you tell your reader who it was and when they said it. There are two ways that you might communicate this information: in your own words, or in the author's words. How do you know which to choose? A good rule of thumb is that in your own words is usually best, unless there's a special reason for using the author's words. Here's an example. You've read three books about the planet Saturn, and learned a lot. What you learned falls into three categories:

1. General knowledge: Saturn is the sixth planet from the sun and has rings. These facts are very commonly known and appear in pretty much anything you'd read about Saturn. You should talk about this information in your own words and don't need to say where you read it.

2. Specific information that may not appear everywhere. For instance, you read in a book that in 1980, the Voyager 1 probe learned a lot about the atmosphere of Saturn's moon Titan. Particularly if you're giving more details about this information, it would be good to put it in your own words,

and then tell where you learned it. A good tip for really getting things in your own words is to write the section without having the author's book or website open in front of you, and then go back to double-check your facts.

3. The author's words are special in some way, because she's talking about her own experience, says something in a unique way, or otherwise makes a real impression. Don't quote just because you think the author writes better than you do! When you're quoting, use quotation marks and indicate the source of the information, including the page number.

Citation: How to Show Where You Got the Information

In the main text of what you write, it's easy to show where you got the information.

- If you're summarizing information, put the author's name and the date in parentheses at the end of the sentence:

> You'd weigh a little bit more on Saturn than you do on earth (Simon, 1985).

The period at the end of the sentence goes after the parentheses.

- If you're quoting exact words, the author, date, and page number go right after the quotation:

> "If you could find an ocean large enough, Saturn would float on the water" (Simon, 1985, p. 12).

- Two special cases:

If it's a website, just put the URL in parentheses:

> (http://nineplanets.org/saturn.html)

If you talked to the person, cite it like this:

> (Seymour Simon, personal communication, April 17, 2012)

References: Full Details of Where You Got the Information

The last page of your informational writing should be a reference list of everything that you read or watched to get information about the topic. You don't need to include websites or personal communication that you already cited in your writing. The page should have the heading *References* and be in alphabetical order by the author's last name. You include, in this order:

Author's name, last name first

Date, including the issue date for magazines

Title (book's title, or both the article and the magazine it's in)

Place (city only, except include the state if it's not a big city) and **Publisher** for books

Here are examples of a book and a magazine article. You should follow the punctuation in these examples exactly. Capitalize the major words in titles of magazines, but not in the titles of magazine articles. If you're writing by hand, use underlining instead of italics.

> Colapinto, John. (2008, April 7). Secrets of the deep. *The New Yorker.*
>
> Simon, Seymour. (1985). *Saturn.* New York: HarperCollins.

For websites you used but didn't cite in the text, use the main name of the website and the URL:

> Nine planets. http://nineplanets.org/saturn.html

For other sources, like TV shows or museum visits, ask your teacher how to cite and reference them.

Annotations: Telling More About Your Sources

Sometimes authors will create annotated reference lists or bibliographies. These include a sentence or two about each source that tell readers more about why they might want to read it themselves. For instance, an annotation for Seymour Simon's Saturn book might say, "A good overview of important information about Saturn, with spectacular photos, although there are newer books available."

Appendix D: Annotated Bibliographies

Reference Books for Students and Adults

In any bookstore with a big children's section, you'll find a number of dictionaries and thesauruses for students of various ages. I recommend both Scholastic's and Merriam-Webster's. You should plan to buy at least one copy of a dictionary for at least one level younger than your students, since it will be easier to navigate for less proficient students. Merriam-Webster is the most authoritative source for language reference, both online (http://www.merriam-webster.com/) and in print. The website can be browsed and used to answer reference questions, and has information about buying apps, handheld devices, and electronic books. They have books available in multiple categories, including learner's guides for English language learners. The website also shows a section of "writing guides" that includes both full-size usage and punctuation guides and inexpensive pocket ones, which are especially accessible for middle school students.

Webster's *Collegiate Dictionary* (updated regularly; the latest edition is the 11th) is the best adult dictionary, and I'd recommend one for every classroom so that students can find less common words and research word origins. Its parent book is *Webster's Third New International Dictionary*, expensive and huge but wonderful. If classrooms don't have it, the school library should. The best comprehensive usage book is *Garner's Modern American Usage* (2009), as mentioned throughout this book: very detailed and perhaps appealing to some older students, and definitive when talking about language change and acceptability.

There are a lot of usage guides for adults that are designed to be more appealing than the more formal guides, which you can find by browsing in the reference section of a bookstore or in a search on amazon.com, but most of them contain the same information as the more formal ones. I do like Grammar Girl's books and website, however, and June Casagrande has a more irreverent and contemporary approach than most. (See Casagrande and Fogarty in this book's reference list.) A warning, however: don't be tempted to buy, as I was, *The Elements of F*cking Style: A Helpful Parody*. It's too vulgar to be funny, and is riddled with incorrect grammatical advice. I also can't recommend Strunk and White's classic *Elements of Style*; it's old-fashioned and has been roundly criticized by linguists as not being very good or accurate.

Books for Teachers About Teaching Grammar and Related Topics

Often books about teaching grammar are very traditional; this list is made up of books that are contemporary in their approaches; they mainly deal with writing mechanics and other practical applications of grammatical content. Rather than doing full annotations, I've provided tags that will help you decide whether to check out the book online to see if it might be useful for you.

Anderson, Jeff. (2005). *Mechanically inclined: Building grammar, usage, and style into writer's workshop.* Portland, ME: Stenhouse Publishers. Grades 4–8, writer's craft, lots of lessons.

Angelillo, Janet. (2008). *Grammar study: Helping students get what grammar is and how it works.* New York: Scholastic. Grades 3–6; traditional grammar topics; nontraditional approach grounded in developing kids' thinking.

Angelillo, Janet, & Calkins, Lucy M. (2002). *A fresh approach to teaching punctuation: Helping young writers use conventions with precision and purpose.* New York: Scholastic Professional Books. Grades 2–5; punctuation; nontraditional approach grounded in developing kids' thinking.

Ehrenworth, Mary, & Vinton, Vicki. (2005). *The power of grammar: Unconventional approaches to the conventions of language.* Portsmouth, NH: Heinemann. Grades 5–9; terminology and mechanics; units of study.

Feigelson, Daniel H. (2008). *Practical punctuation: Lessons on rule making and rule breaking in elementary writing.* Portsmouth, NH: Heinemann. Grades K–6; punctuation; lessons grounded in reading and writing workshop.

Francois, Chantal, & Zonana, Elisa. (2009). *Catching up on conventions: Grammar lessons for middle school writers.* Portsmouth, NH: Heinemann. Grades 6–9; conventions and code-switching; contemporary approach with special emphasis on AAVE.

Goodman, Yetta M. (2003). *Valuing language study: Inquiry into language for elementary and middle schools.* Urbana, IL: National Council of Teachers of English. Grades K–9; linguistic and social orientation; understanding children's language use and helping them explore language.

Schuster, Edgar H. (2003). *Breaking the rules: Liberating writers through innovative grammar instruction.* Portsmouth, NH: Heinemann. Grades 6–12; traditional grammar and usage topics; contemporary and linguistically accurate lessons.

Weaver, Constance. (1996). *Teaching grammar in context.* Portsmouth, NH: Boynton/Cook Publishers. Grades 6–12; traditional grammar topics; an important reconceptualization by a leader in the field, with sample lessons.

Weaver, Constance. (1998). *Lessons to share on teaching grammar in context.* Portsmouth, NH: Boynton/Cook. Grades 6–12; multiple aspects of grammar; an edited collection.

Weaver, Constance. (2007). *The grammar plan book: A guide to smart teaching.* Portsmouth, NH: Heinemann. Grades 6–12; grammar and mechanics; a collection of lessons.

Weaver, Constance. (2008). *Grammar to enrich & enhance writing.* Portsmouth, NH: Heinemann. Grades 6–12; grammar and mechanics; developed around 12 fresh principles for instruction.

Wheeler, Rebecca S., & Swords, Rachel. (2006). *Code-switching: Teaching Standard English in urban classrooms.* Urbana, IL: National Council of Teachers of English. Grades K–6; code-switching for students in urban classrooms; background and teaching ideas.

Wheeler, Rebecca S., & Swords, Rachel. (2010). *Code-switching lessons: Grammar strategies for linguistically diverse writers.* Portsmouth, NH: Heinemann. Grades 3–6; code-switching for speakers of AAVE and other varieties of English; nine units of study, with accompanying DVD.

Books for Teachers About Linguistics

I've read a lot of books about linguistics; here I've worked to choose a dozen that are likely to be of the most interest for general readers, some of them referenced elsewhere in this book. They're mostly nontechnical or only difficult in parts; I've also selected them to represent a range of topics. I've chosen them not for their practical use for teaching purposes but as a curated reading list for those who'd like to learn more about language because of their own interest in the topic. They're all aimed at general, nonscholarly audiences, not teachers specifically. Most of them include some linguistic detail, but all of the books can be appreciated without understanding all of the linguistics. I've also included as wide a range of topics as possible, hoping that everyone will find at least one book of interest.

Anderson, Stephen R. (2004). *Doctor Dolittle's delusion: Animals and the uniqueness of human language*. New Haven: Yale University Press.

We know that animals communicate, but do they have languages? Anderson writes a great deal about the (failed) primate language experiments, but also examines communication among the birds and the bees and other animals. One of his interesting insights is that the attempts to teach language to nonhuman primates may well have been a distraction from the more interesting topics of animals' own communication systems.

Austin, Peter. (2008). *1000 languages: The worldwide history of living and lost tongues*. London: Thames & Hudson.

I'd recommend this beautifully designed and illustrated book for those who are interested in language in all its diverse global splendor. The book starts with profiles of 11 world languages, then includes interesting information on the languages of each region of the world, ending with chapters on endangered and extinct languages. All of the authors are academic linguists, so the book is authoritative, but it's designed for the general reader. It's more for browsing in than for reading beginning to end.

Bickerton, Derek. (2008). *Bastard tongues: A trailblazing linguist finds clues to our common humanity in the world's lowliest languages*. New York: Hill & Wang.

Bickerton has written a number of books, but I'm recommending this one because it's a memoir as well as a book on language and linguistics. He begins the book with a story about drinking in a bar in Guyana and the linguistic insight found in a comment from a passerby, and fills the book with stories of his travels all over the world exploring Creole languages. It's also a great history and geography story about how colonized and enslaved people have developed language over the past several centuries.

Dillard, J. L. (1973; 1972). *Black English: Its history and usage in the United States*. New York: Vintage Books.

Of the many excellent books about African American Vernacular English, I'm recommending this older one because of its importance and authoritativeness. When I read it in the 1970s, I was stunned by what I learned from it, that AAVE has a history deeply grounded in the social and linguistic environment of slavery in the Americas, as well as a distinct grammatical structure. Writing at a time when the predominant educational model for thinking about AAVE was a deficit one, Dillard confronted prejudices and prevailing practices with a clear blast of knowledge. No longer in print, but available cheaply on Amazon.

Everett, Daniel L. (2008). *Don't sleep, there are snakes: Life and language in the Amazonian jungle* (1st ed.). New York: Pantheon Books.

Like Bickerton's *Bastard Tongues*, this book combines linguistics and travelogue. Everett and his family spent seven years living with the Pirahã tribe in Brazil, and theorized (controversially) that their language has significant differences from others that require adjustments in linguistic theory. But readers will be mostly fascinated by his experiences living in this community, including the loss of his Christian religious faith.

Fox, Margalit. (2007). *Talking hands: What sign language reveals about the mind*. New York: Simon & Schuster.

The best book I've read about the history and linguistics of sign, combined with Fox's journalistic account of a remote Bedouin community in Israel whose newly developed sign is being studied by a team of linguists. The book is solidly researched but completely accessible to the general reader.

Greene, Robert L. (2011). *You are what you speak: Grammar grouches, language laws, and the politics of identity.* New York: Delacorte Press.

An up-to-date look at the diversity, culture, and politics of language around the world. Greene, a journalist, writes about "grammar grouches" and other judgments of language and, most interestingly, language policies and politics: attempts to legislate and control national languages, and to enforce language policies, and how these come up against language as a living badge of identity that won't let itself be suppressed.

Kaplan, Justin, & Bernays, Anne. (1997). *The language of names.* New York: Simon & Schuster.

The Language of Names is both thought-provoking and a lot of fun. Serious topics like the histories of proper names among Jews and African Americans are followed by discussions of which names work only for one gender or for both, changing your name (when you get married? if you become an actor?), and even the names of literary characters. A light read that really gets you thinking, which might spark ideas for exploring with students.

Lynch, Jack. (2009). *The lexicographer's dilemma: The evolution of "proper" English, from Shakespeare to South Park.* New York: Walker & Co.

Most of this book is for history buffs, as the subtitle indicates, but it's fascinating to see that grammarians have been complaining about other people's English for like, forever. The new generation is always making changes in the way they speak, and the older generation fights it until they (inevitably) lose.

McWhorter, John H. (2011). *What language is: And what it isn't and what it could be.* New York: Gotham Books.

McWhorter's several books on language for nontechnical audiences are all wonderful. I've chosen to highlight his newest one here. His chapters on language as being ingrown, disheveled, intricate, oral, and mixed draw on examples from all over the world (with maps) to show us how the world's diverse languages all share common principles that play out in all kinds of ways. He includes a good section on AAVE.

Perry, Theresa, & Delpit, Lisa D. (1998). *The real Ebonics debate: Power, language, and the education of African-American children.* Boston: Beacon Press.

This book is essential reading for teachers of African American students or anyone who wonders what the Ebonics debate was all about and what grew out of it. In 1996, the Oakland, CA Board of Education passed a resolution intended to support the language development of the district's children. It was widely misinterpreted and criticized. This book not only sets the record straight but clarifies important principles for working with speakers of AAVE (the word *Ebonics* is rarely used in serious discussion anymore) in the classroom.

Yang, Charles D. (2006). *The infinite gift: How children learn and unlearn the languages of the world.* New York: Scribner.

Yang's book helps the general reader understand in detail how children learn to talk: the sounds, the words, the sentences, the ideas, all around the world, in whatever language. It gets a little technical in spots, but the depth of explanation can be very valuable for teachers (parents too!) to understand how complex and astonishing language acquisition is.

Books for Kids About Grammar and Conventions

These include books with a pedagogical intent and those that are more for developing an interest in language; I've included both those that I think are good and a few that are widely known but perhaps should be avoided.

PARTS OF SPEECH

There are three excellent sets of books for individual parts of speech; I've discussed them in order of when they were first published, oldest first. For students in grades 3–5, I'd recommend buying one of the sets as a support for whatever discussion you do with them about understanding the parts of speech. You don't need to spend a lot of time on the topic, and these books expose kids to the definitions and rules pretty painlessly.

Heller, Ruth. (1987). *A cache of jewels and other collective nouns*. New York: Grosset & Dunlap.

Heller, Ruth. (1988). *Kites sail high: A book about verbs*. New York: Grosset & Dunlap.

Heller, Ruth. (1989). *Many luscious lollipops: A book about adjectives*. New York: Grosset & Dunlap.

Heller, Ruth. (1990). *Merry-go-round: A book about nouns*. New York: Grosset & Dunlap.

Heller, Ruth. (1995). *Behind the mask: A book about prepositions*. New York: Grosset & Dunlap.

Heller, Ruth. (1997). *Mine, all mine: A book about pronouns*. New York: Grosset & Dunlap.

Heller, Ruth. (1998). *Fantastic! wow! and unreal!: A book about interjections and conjunctions*. New York: Grosset & Dunlap.

The late Ruth Heller first had the idea of doing picture books about the parts of speech, and this series is splendidly realized. She also illustrated Merriam-Webster's *Alphabet Book* and *First Dictionary*, both of which I highly recommend. The illustrations in her parts-of-speech books are absolutely stunning; the text is rhymed and perhaps a little heavy-handed in places, since it tries to cover all the rules. ("Despite what you have heard, PREPOSITIONS can be more than one word.")

Cleary, Brian P. (1999). *A mink, a fink, a skating rink: What is a noun?* Minneapolis: Carolrhoda Books.

Cleary, Brian P. (2000). *Hairy, scary, ordinary: What is an adjective?* Minneapolis: Carolrhoda Books.

Cleary, Brian P. (2001). *To root, to toot, to parachute: What is a verb?* Minneapolis: Carolrhoda Books.

Cleary, Brian P. (2002). *Under, over, by the clover: What is a preposition?* Minneapolis: Carolrhoda Books.

Cleary, Brian P. (2003). *Dearly, nearly, insincerely: What is an adverb?* Minneapolis: Carolrhoda Books.

Cleary, Brian P. (2004). *I and you and don't forget who: What is a pronoun?* Minneapolis: Carolrhoda Books.

Cleary, Brian P. (2010). *But and for, yet and nor: What is a conjunction?* Minneapolis: Millbrook Press.

Cleary, Brian P. (2011). *Cool! whoa! ah! and oh!: What is an interjection?* Minneapolis: Millbrook Press.

Brian Cleary's books are the simplest of these three sets; I'd recommend them especially for third-graders who just need a relatively simple introduction to parts of speech.

Dahl, Michael, & Loewen, Nancy. (2009). *If you were a noun, a verb, an adjective, an adverb, a pronoun, a conjunction, an interjection, a preposition.* Minneapolis: Picture Window Books.

Dahl wrote some books on individual parts of speech, but I'd recommend instead this compendium, which includes the contents of the earlier books and more, so that it includes all the parts of speech. The text is simpler and less comprehensive than Heller's books, with a little more linguistic analysis and some "fun with" activities for each part of speech, such as acting out prepositions. Both Cleary and Dahl have written other books about language, on topics such as homophones and synonyms, but I've included here only the ones on parts of speech. Their other language books are similar in style and quality.

OTHER TECHNICAL LANGUAGE TOPICS

Pulver, Robin. (2003). *Punctuation takes a vacation* (1st ed.). New York: Holiday House.

Pulver, Robin. (2006). *Nouns and verbs have a field day* (1st ed.). New York: Holiday House.

Pulver, Robin. (2008). *Silent letters loud and clear* (1st ed.). New York: Holiday House.

Pulver, Robin. (2011). *Happy endings: A story about suffixes* (1st ed.). New York: Holiday House.

Pulver, Robin. (2012). *The case of the incapacitated capitals* (1st ed.). New York: Holiday House.

Robin Pulver has created a charming series of books in which grammatical and writing mechanics features are personified and made into stories. I wouldn't use them above third grade, since they're definitely in a younger picture-book style, but they're worth taking a look at to see if they'd provide new knowledge at a level appropriate for your students.

Truss, Lynne, & Timmons, Bonnie. (2006). *Eats, shoots & leaves: Why, commas really do make a difference!* New York: G. P. Putnam's Sons.

Truss, Lynne, & Timmons, Bonnie. (2007). *The girl's like spaghetti: Why, you can't manage without apostrophes!* New York: G. P. Putnam's Sons.

Truss, Lynne, & Timmons, Bonnie. (2008). *Twenty-odd ducks: Why, every punctuation mark counts!* New York: G. P. Putnam's Sons.

I can't recommend Lynne Truss's children's books, which grew out of her adult bestseller *Eats, Shoots & Leaves*, although they're popular and nicely illustrated. Her examples are often forced (contrasting "students' refuse," meaning their trash, with "students refuse," with *refuse* as a noun) and sometimes not really accurate. Even her adult book is also problematic; she comes from the "picky grammarian" school rather than from good contemporary knowledge about language. If you use the children's books, since they do give examples how a punctuation mark can affect meaning, be aware that most but not all of her examples are good ones.

Books for Kids: Thinking and Learning About Language

I focus here on books that represent a range of topics. There are now many language books for kids, a lot of them similar to each other. I've included some of these, but have also singled out a number that are notable in some way, such as the unusualness of the topic or their quality. I believe that

these books would make for an excellent small linguistics collection for a
school or classroom library.

Bruno, Elsa K., & Whitehead, Jenny. (2009). *Punctuation celebration* (1st ed.).
New York: Henry Holt & Co.

Carr, Jan, & Long, Ethan. (2007). *Greedy apostrophe: A cautionary tale* (1st
ed.). New York: Holiday House.

Donohue, Moira R., & Adinolfi, JoAnn. (2006). *Alfie the apostrophe*. Morton
Grove, IL: Albert Whitman.

Donohue, Moira R., & Law, Jenny. (2008). *Penny and the punctuation bee*.
Morton Grove, IL: Albert Whitman.

These four books represent a mini-bandwagon of books on punctuation
mechanics for kids. All four are cute, fun picture books where punctuation marks are explored in a lively, brightly illustrated manner. They
don't, however, substitute for good, focused, interactive teaching on how
to punctuate; think of them as more for creating interest than for teaching. These aren't the first books I'd choose for the classroom library;
they're also too young for middle school.

Clements, Andrew. (1997). *Double trouble in walla walla*. Brookfield, CT:
Millbrook Press.

Shulman, Mark. (2006). *Mom and dad are palindromes: A dilemma for words-
backwards*. San Francisco: Chronicle Books.

These two books, by different authors but similar, are basically
language-play stories. Clements' very funny book is about a kid who
can't help spouting sing-songy words and phrases ("Ship-shape sump-
pump! Achey-breaky doodad!"). Shulman's book has a child who goes
similarly nuts over palindromes, words and phrases spelled the same
backwards and forwards. No teaching in these books, just fun. I'd recommend both for their clever premises and execution.

Day, Alexandra. (1988). *Frank and Ernest*. New York: Scholastic.

Day, Alexandra. (1990). *Frank and Ernest play ball*. New York: Scholastic.

Day, Alexandra. (1994). *Frank and Ernest on the road*. New York: Scholastic.

> This set of books sees Frank and Ernest (a bear and elephant, respectively) take on temporary jobs at a diner, on a baseball team, and driving trucks, where they learn the special lingo of each job, such as "Adam and Eve on a raft" for two poached eggs on toast. Although the books are designed for younger children, they'd be an interesting introduction for all ages to the world of specialized vocabulary that grows up in workplace settings.

Disch, Thomas M., & Morice, Dave. (1997). *A child's garden of grammar*. Hanover, NH: University Press of New England.

> This unusual book is written by a well-known (adult) science-fiction author, illustrated by the creator of *Poetry Comics*, and published by a university press. The table of contents is made up of grammar terminology, but each topic is a poem, a comic, or both. For instance: "If/Then is a wonderful machine/If you use soap, then you'll be clean." It's not a beginner's guide but rather commentary on these grammatical topics. Don't miss it, especially for middle school.

Dubosarsky, Ursula. (2009). *The word snoop*. New York: Dial Books.

> There are many books for adults about exploring language in playful ways; this one is targeted to grades 5–8. It's full of interesting facts about words, ideas for wordplay, and up-to-date information about texting conventions and other new forms of written communication.

Gerstein, Mordicai. (1998). *The wild boy* (1st ed.). New York: Farrar, Straus & Giroux.

> The true story of the "Wild Boy of Aveyron," a feral child who was discovered in France in 1800. Although it's a picture book, it's informative for

students in higher grades. It raises interesting questions about what language is and how children acquire it; Victor's story was also made into a feature film (in French with English subtitles) by Fran ois Truffaut, *The Wild Child* (1970); it's rated G and appropriate for kids, and watching a film with subtitles might be a new and enjoyable experience for them.

Noble, Trinka H., & Kellogg, Steven. (1980). *The day jimmy's boa ate the wash.* New York: Dial Press.

Noble, Trinka H., & Kellogg, Steven. (1984). *Jimmy's boa bounces back* (1st ed.). New York: Dial Books for Young Readers.

Noble, Trinka H., & Kellogg, Steven. (1989). *Jimmy's boa and the big splash birthday bash* (1st ed.). New York: Dial Books for Young Readers.

Noble, Trinka H., & Kellogg, Steven. (2003). *Jimmy's boa and the bungee jump slam dunk.* New York: Dial Books for Young Readers.

These well-known picture books feature a child's rendition to a parent of a day that gets more and more out of control, with pictures that show how crazy it really got. What makes them interesting linguistically is that they're told entirely in dialogue, with quotation marks—not a single "he said" to carry the dialogue. As an introduction to how dialogue is punctuated, these books could be contrasted with regular dialogue in books as well as play scripts.

Rumford, James. (2004). *Sequoyah: The Cherokee man who gave his people writing.* Boston: Houghton Mifflin.

This solidly researched book is written in both English and Cherokee, providing readers with not only the important story of a man who invented a written form of his community's language but information about the language itself and exposure to both characters and text in a completely different writing system. A picture book biography that's appropriate for all ages.

Robb, Don. (2007). *Ox, house, stick: The history of our alphabet.* Watertown, MA: Charlesbridge.

A well-researched and engaging book by an author of other history books for children that takes the reader through the history of our alphabet letter by letter. It's an illustrated book that would be informative for middle school as well as elementary, since the information is so solid and complete.

Samoyault, Tiphaine. (1997). *Give me a sign!: What pictograms tell us without words* [Monde des pictogrammes]. New York: Viking.

Samoyault, Tiphaine. (1998). *Alphabetical order: How the alphabet began* [Monde des alphabets]. New York: Viking.

These two books, translated from French, are very informative accounts, written in topical chapters such as "The World's Alphabets" and "Everyday Pictograms." They're short and heavily illustrated, but are informational books for middle grades, not picture books, and are especially valuable for packing a lot of research into just 32 pages each.

Appendix E: Literature in Different Versions of American English

Is It Authentic?

Literature as diverse as *Huckleberry Finn, Their Eyes Were Watching God,* and *The Brief Wondrous Life of Oscar Wao* has represented the versions of English spoken by different communities of Americans. This is also increasingly true of children's books. Here I'd like to present a brief guide for judging whether such language representation is authentic or not. I'm going to focus primarily on African American Vernacular English, since it's the version most commonly represented in children's literature, but similar principles apply for other American Englishes.

The Uncle Remus stories retold by Joel Chandler Harris a century ago (see www.gutenberg.org for examples) used a broad representation of Southern Black English that now feels offensive and inauthentic to us: "Once 'pon a time Mr. Man had a gyarden so fine dat all de neighbors come ter see it." Today, we need better examples. For instance, Julius Lester, a contemporary African American author, created new versions of these stories for today's audiences beginning in 1987, using more natural and realistic language for these characters. The great African American writer Langston Hughes used different versions of English in different poems: "The Negro Speaks of Rivers" includes the lines, "I bathed in the Euphrates when dawns were young./I built my hut near the Congo and it lulled me to sleep." In "Homesick Blues," he writes "To keep from cryin'/I opens ma mouth and laughs" (both published in the 1920s). His use of both kinds of English authentically showcases his use of different registers depending on his intentions.

The first question to ask in choosing books with diverse language is whether the author is from the culture whose language is being represented. Many recent Black authors have made an explicit choice to represent their culture's language in literature for children, especially in dialogue or with first-person narrators. *Stevie* (Steptoe, 1969) is an early example: "Sometimes people get on your nerves and they don't mean it or nothin', but they just bother you. Why I gotta put up with him?" Sometimes a little research can discover if the author's background qualifies them to write in this version of English. For instance, *Possum Come a-Knockin'* (Van Laan, 1990), a brief picture book written in verse with strong Appalachian features, includes a dedication to the author's "kinfolk way down South."

If the author isn't from a culture and uses features from its language in a book, particularly in the mouths of characters, you can not only try to find out about the author's background but look at book reviews to see if there are comments about authenticity. Amazon's many reader reviews are sometimes useful in catching problems. Readers can also develop an ear for what sounds right and what doesn't. I offer here an extended comparison between two books, *Elijah of Buxton* (Curtis, 2007) and *The Help* (Stockett, 2009). The former, by the African American author Christopher Paul Curtis, is set in a Canadian community of former slaves in the 1800s. Leonard Marcus' book of interviews with children's authors, *Funny Business* (2009) contains a facsimile of an edited manuscript page from Curtis' book (p. 62). The following lines appear in the final book (p. 17):

"Yes, ma'am, she told me to ask 'bout you."

"Mrs. Brown come by, axed if you's gunn go fishing tomorrow."

In the facsimile page, we can see where the copy editor has apparently made check marks on AAVE features and made some changes in them, and then Curtis' responses. In the first line above, the editor had changed *ask* to *ax*, but then Curtis changed it back again. Similar edits occur elsewhere on the page. Curtis and his editor were clearly working very precisely to represent the language of two characters of different ages precisely and with nuance.

By contrast, look at a randomly chosen passage of narration by an African American housekeeper in 1962 Mississippi written by Kathryn Stockett, a Southern white author: "None a the Medgar Evers talk come up in Miss Leefolt's house. I change the station when she come back from her lunch meeting. We go on like it's a nice summer afternoon. I still ain't heard hide nor hair from Miss Hilly and I'm sick a the worry that's always in my head" (p. 232). I've been unable to read this popular and controversial book because the language just rings so false to me. It feels as if the author (or a copy editor) went through and changed *of* to *a* and past-tense verbs to present tense, and inserted *ain't* and quaint expressions like *hide nor hair* whenever possible. The next page includes the expressions *I spec, her own self, evertime,* and *granmama.* The main white character's narration doesn't even seem to have a Southern accent. I rest my case.

I include here a brief selection of books that represent African American dialect especially well. I've chosen picture books since they're of a length that can be read quickly and then used as a basis for discussing features of the language. You'll also, of course, want to seek out good examples in fiction for students in grades 3–8; any well-reviewed novel by an African American author is likely to include AAVE in dialogue and first-person narration.

Jump at the sun treasury: An African American picture book collection (2001). New York: Jump at the Sun/Hyperion Books for Children. An anthology of seven previously published books, some for younger readers, some for older, with a variety of language use represented. Now out of print, but available at bargain prices online.

McKissack, Patricia. (1986). *Flossie & the fox.* New York: Dial Books for Young Readers. Set in the rural South some years ago. Notice the differences between Flossie's language and the fox's, and think about why the fox uses more formal language.

McKissack, Patricia. (2000). *The honest-to-goodness truth.* New York: Atheneum Books. This picture-book story of a girl grappling with the subtle social effects of always telling the truth includes some nice language variation across both Black and White characters, including a teacher's grammatical correction of "Willie don't got his geography homework" being interpreted by the character as an affirmation of the sentence's truth.

Smalls, Irene. (1991). *Irene and the big, fine nickel.* Boston: Little, Brown. Just a great story of four young girls speaking their own language and enjoying a sunny day in Harlem.

Aboff, Marcie. (2008). *If you were a suffix*. North Mankato, MN: Picture Window.

American Heritage. (2004). *100 words almost everyone confuses and misuses*. Boston: Houghton Mifflin.

Angelillo, Janet. (2002). *A fresh approach to teaching punctuation: Helping young writers use conventions with precision and purpose*. New York: Scholastic.

Atkinson, Quentin D. (2011). Phonemic diversity supports a serial founder effect model of language expansion from Africa. *Science, 332*, 346–349.

Baugh, John. (2003). Linguistic profiling, in Makoni, Sinfree, Smitherman, Geneva, Ball, Arnetha F., & Spears, Arthur K. (Eds.). *Black linguistics: Language, society, and politics in Africa and the Americas*. New York: Routledge, pp. 155–163.

Bickerton, Derek. (2008). *Bastard tongues: A trailblazing linguist finds clues to our common humanity in the world's lowliest languages*. New York: Hill & Wang.

Calkins, Lucy. (1980). When children want to punctuate: Basic skills belong in context. *Language Arts, 57*, 567–573.

Cary, Stephen. (2007). *Working with English language learners: Answers to teachers' top ten questions* (2nd ed.). Portsmouth, NH: Heinemann.

Casagrande, June. (2006). *Grammar snobs are great big meanies: A guide to language for fun and spite.* New York: Penguin.

Casagrande, June. (2008). *Mortal syntax: 101 language choices that will get you clobbered by the grammar snobs—even if you're right.* New York: Penguin.

Chang, Kenneth. (2011, June 16). Close up, Mercury is looking less boring. *New York Times.* (Retrieved electronically).

Charity Hudley, Anne H., & Mallinson, Christine. (2011). *Understanding English language variation in U.S. schools.* New York: Teachers College.

Chomsky, Noam. (1957). *Syntactic structures.* The Hague: Mouton.

Chomsky, Noam. (2010). Some simple evo devo theses: How true might they be for language? In Richard K. Larson, Viviane D prez, & Hiroko Yamakido (Eds.). *The Evolution of human language: Biolinguistic perspectives* (Approaches to the Evolution of Language) (pp. 45–62). New York: Cambridge University Press.

Churchill, Caryl. (1984). *Top girls.* London: Methuen.

Clements, Andrew. (1996). *Frindle.* New York: Simon & Schuster.

Comrie, Bernard, Matthews, Stephen, & Polinsky, Maria. (2003). *The atlas of languages: The origin and development of languages throughout the world* (Facts on File Library of Language and Literature Series). New York: Checkmark.

Cran, William. (2005). *Do you speak American?* [DVD]. Princeton, NJ: Films for the Humanities & Sciences.

Crystal, David. (2010). *Evolving English: One language, many voices: An illustrated history of the English language.* London: British Library.

Davies, Nicola. (2006). *Extreme animals: The toughest creatures on earth.* Somerville, MA: Candlewick.

Delpit, Lisa, & Dowdy, Joanne K. (Eds.) (2002). *The skin that we speak: Thoughts on language and culture in the classroom.* New York: New Press.

Delpit, Lisa. (1995). *Other people's children: Cultural conflict in the classroom.* New York: The New Press.

Dowd, Maureen. (2011, July 5). The Twitter zone. *New York Times.* (Retrieved electronically).

Elley, W. B., Barham, I. H., Lamb, H., & Wyllie, M. (1975). The role of grammar in a secondary school English curriculum. *New Zealand Journal of Educational Studies, 10,* 26–42.

Fertig, Beth. (2009). *Why cant U teach me 2 read?: Three students and a mayor put our schools to the test.* New York: Farrar, Straus & Giroux.

Florey, Kitty B. (2006). *Sister Bernadette's barking dog: The quirky history and lost art of diagramming sentences.* Hoboken, NJ: Melville House.

Florey, Kitty B. (2009). *Script and scribble: The rise and fall of handwriting.* Hoboken, NJ: Melville House.

Fogarty, Mignon. (2011). *Grammar Girl's 101 misused words you'll never confuse again.* New York: St. Martin's Griffin.

Francois, Chantal, & Zonana, Elisa. (2009). *Catching up on conventions: Grammar lessons for middle school writers.* Portsmouth, NH: Heinemann.

Garfield, Simon. (2011). *Just my type: A book about fonts.* New York: Gotham.

Garner, Bryan A. (2009). *Garner's modern American usage.* New York: Oxford University Press.

Goodman, Kenneth S. (1969). Analysis of oral reading miscues: Applied psycholinguistics. *Reading Research Quarterly, 5,* 9–30.

Goodman, Yetta M., & Wilde, Sandra. (Eds.) (1992). *Literacy events in a community of young writers.* New York: Teachers College.

Grant, Gerald. (2009). *Hope and despair in the American city: Why there are no bad schools in Raleigh.* Cambridge, MA: Harvard University Press.

Harrison, K. David. (2010). *The last speakers: The quest to save the world's most endangered languages.* Washington, DC: National Geographic.

Harshaw, Tobin. (2008, Oct. 10). It ain't over. *New York Times.* (Retrieved electronically).

Hauser, Marc D., Chomsky, Noam, & Fitch, W. Tecumseh. (2002). The faculty of language: What is it, who has it, and how did it evolve? *Science, 298,* 1569–1579.

Heller, Lora. (2004). *Sign language for kids: A fun & easy guide to American Sign Language.* New York: Sterling.

Hess, Elizabeth. (2008). *Nim Chimpsky: The chimp who would be human.* New York: Bantam.

Hillocks, Jr., George. (1987). Synthesis of research on teaching writing. *Educational Leadership, 44,* 71–82.

Huddleston, Rodney D., & Pullum, Geoffrey K. (2002). *The Cambridge grammar of the English language.* New York: Cambridge University Press.

Hunt, Kellogg W. (1965). *Grammatical structures written at three grade levels.* Champaign, IL, National Council of Teachers of English.

Isadora, Rachel. (2007). *Yo, Jo!* New York: Harcourt.

Jablonski, Nina G., & Chaplin, George. (2000). The evolution of human skin coloration. *Journal of Human Evolution, 39,* 57–106.

Jochnowitz, George. (1983). Another view of *you guys. American Speech, 58,* 68–70.

Klein, William L. (1916). *Why we punctuate: Or, reason versus rule in the use of marks.* Minneapolis: Lancet.

Klima, Edward S., & Bellugi, Ursula. (1979). *The signs of language.* Cambridge, MA: Harvard University Press.

Krashen, Stephen D. (1981). *Second language acquisition and second language learning.* New York: Pergamon Press.

Krashen, Stephen D. (1982). *Principles and practice in second language acquisition.* New York: Pergamon.

Krashen, Stephen D. (2004). *The power of reading: Insights from the research.* (2nd ed.). Portsmouth, NH: Heinemann.

Krashen, Stephen D. (2011). *Free voluntary reading.* Santa Barbara, CA: Libraries Unlimited.

Labov, William, & Harris, Wendell A. (1986). De facto segregation of black and white vernaculars. In Sankoff, David. (Ed.) *Diversity and diachrony.* Amsterdam ; Philadelphia, Pa.: John Benjamins. Pp. 1–24.

Leonard, Elmore. (2001, July 16). Writers on writing: Easy on the adverbs, exclamation points and especially hooptedoodle. *New York Times.* (Retrieved electronically).

MacNeil, Robert, & Cran, William. (2005). *Do you speak American?* New York: Doubleday.

McCrum, Robert. (2010). *Globish: How the English language became the world's language.* New York: W. W. Norton.

McIntosh, Peggy. (1990). White privilege: Unpacking the invisible knapsack. *Independent School, 49,* 31–35.

McWhorter, John. (1998). *Word on the street: Debunking the myth of "pure" standard English.* Cambridge, MA: Perseus.

Merriam-Webster. (1989). *The Merriam-Webster Dictionary of English Usage.* Springfield, MA: Merriam-Webster.

Merriam-Webster's Pocket Guide to Punctuation. (2001). Springfield, MA: Merriam-Webster.

Mukherjee, Siddhartha. (2010). *The emperor of all maladies: A biography of cancer.* New York: Scribner.

Nettle, Daniel. (2000). *Vanishing voices: The extinction of the world's languages.* New York: Oxford.

Noble, Trinka H. (1992). *The day Jimmy's boa ate the wash.* New York: Puffin.

Ogbu, John U. (1978). *Minority education and caste: The American system in cross-cultural perspective.* New York: Academic Press.

Ogbu, John U. (2003). *Black American students in an affluent suburb: A study of academic disengagement.* Mahwah, NJ: Erlbaum.

Patterson, Francine. (1987). *Koko's kitten.* New York: Scholastic.

Patterson, Francine. (1988). *Koko's story.* New York: Scholastic.

Pinker, Steven. (1995). *The language instinct: How the mind creates language.* New York: Harper Perennial.

Remnick, David. (2011, February 14). Judgment days. *The New Yorker.* Retrieved electronically.

Rumford, James. (2004). *Sequoyah: The Cherokee man who gave his people writing.* Boston: Houghton Mifflin.

Samoyault, Tiphaine. (1997). *Give me a sign!: What pictograms tell us without words.* New York: Viking.

Samoyault, Tiphaine. (1998). *Alphabetical order.* New York: Viking.

Schuster, Edgar H. (2003). *Breaking the rules: Liberating writers through innovative grammar instruction*. Portsmouth, NH: Heinemann.

Scieszka, Jon. (1998). Design matters. *Horn Book, 74*, 196–209.

Selznick, Brian. (2011). *Wonderstruck*. New York: Scholastic.

Smalls, Irene. (2003). *Don't say ain't*. Watertown, MA: Charlesbridge.

Taylor, Kathe, & Walton, Sherry. (1998). *Children at the center: A workshop approach to standardized test preparation, K–8*. Portsmouth, NH: Heinemann.

Van Laan, Nancy. (1992). *Possum come a-knockin'.* New York: Dragonfly.

Walton, Rick. (1997). *Pig, Pigger, Piggest*. Salt Lake City: Gibbs-Smith.

Weaver, Constance. (1996). *Teaching grammar in context*. Portsmouth, NH: Heinemann.

Weaver, Constance. (1998). *Lessons to share on teaching grammar in context*. Portsmouth, NH: Heinemann.

Weaver, Constance. (2006). *The grammar plan book*. Portsmouth, NH: Heinemann.

Weaver, Constance. (2008). *Grammar to enrich and enhance writing*. Portsmouth, NH: Heinemann.

Wells, Spencer. (2010). *Pandora's seed: The unforeseen costs of civilization*. New York: Random House.

Wheeler, Rebecca S., & Swords, Rachel. (2008). *Code-switching: Teaching standard English in urban classrooms*. Urbana, IL: National Council of Teachers of English.

Wilde, Sandra. (1992). *You kan red this!: Spelling and punctuation for whole language classrooms, K–6*. Portsmouth, NH: Heinemann.

Wilde, Sandra. (1997). *What's a schwa sound anyway?: A holistic guide to phonetics, phonics, and spelling*. Portsmouth, NH: Heinemann.

Wilde, Sandra. (2008). *Spelling strategies and patterns: What kids need to know*. Portsmouth, NH: Heinemann.